COLOR

IDEA BOOK

COLOR
IDEA BOOK

ROBIN STRANGIS

The Taunton Press
Inspiration for hands-on living®

The Taunton Press, Inc., 63 South Main Street, PO Box 5506, Newtown, CT 06470-5506
e-mail: tp@taunton.com

Editor: Carolyn Mandarano
Interior design: Susan Fazekas
Interior layout: Cathy Cassidy
Illustrator: Archie Mortera
Front cover photographers: (top row, left to right) Courtesy Stickley Fine Furniture,
© Eric Roth, © Eric Roth, © Steve Vierra; (middle row, left to right) © Eric Roth,
© Bruce Buck, © Eric Roth, © Mike Jensen; (bottom row, left to right) Courtesy the Sherwin
Williams Company, © David Duncan Livingston, © Evan Sklar, © David Duncan Livingston.
Back cover photographrs: (top) © Evan Sklar; (bottom three photos, left to right) © Eric Roth.

Library of Congress Cataloging-in-Publication Data
Strangis, Robin.
  Color idea book / Robin Strangis.
      p. cm.
  ISBN-13: 978-1-56158-914-2
  ISBN-10: 1-56158-914-4
  1. Color in interior decoration. 2. Color decoration and ornament. I. Title.

NK2115.5.C6S88 2007
747'.94--dc22

                                          2006103007

Printed in the United States of America
10 9 8 7 6 5 4 3 2

Acknowledgments

When I was approached last year by Taunton to see if I'd be interested in writing a book on color, my response was "of course!" I had always wanted to write a book and I thought this would be a good opportunity for me. But I realized my limitations as a writer and knew that I would need some help along the way. It reminded me of a quote by Pablo Picasso that I keep on my desk: *"I am always doing things I can't do, that's how I get to do them."* That's me, I thought. While I've always been confident enough to try things I've never done before, I did have my doubts. But after months of pecking away on the computer, with my team of cheerleaders behind me, I completed a book that I'm proud of and that I hope will inspire others. If I hadn't had the help and encouragement of many people, I never could have done it.

First, I owe a big thanks to Heather Paper (another Taunton author), who initially referred me to Taunton Press for this project. A *huge* thanks to Carolyn Mandarano and the talented group at Taunton for giving me this opportunity. Thanks for your confidence in me.

I'd also like to thank Connie Nelson, my editor at the *Minneapolis Star-Tribune* for giving me the opportunity to work with the newspaper on a regular basis. I believe that my experience with the *Star-Tribune* has helped me become a better writer and has opened new doors of opportunity; plus, we have a lot of fun.

Special thanks to the girls at the Kravet showroom in Minneapolis: Patty Scott, the showroom manager; and Amy and Erin, who provided many of the wonderful fabrics shown in this book. (I hope I wasn't too annoying with my daily visits to the showroom. You're the best!)

A heartfelt thanks to my clients, who put up with me during the last several months. Thank you for understanding why I didn't always call you back right away and why your projects took a bit longer than normal to complete. And, thank you for trusting me with the job of decorating your homes. You're not just clients, you're friends. I appreciate all of you!

Finally, I'd like to thank my family: my daughter Jenni, for her computer skills that helped get me through Excel when I didn't know what I was doing; my son Brandon, for his hugs, support, and occasional fast-food runs; and my husband Mark, for keeping the dust under control during our own remodeling project and the daily chore of dealing with contractors who didn't always show up on time. Thanks for always keeping me laughing. I couldn't have done it without you.

I'd like to dedicate this book to everyone who loves color and realizes the awesome and amazing gift of vision and the ability we have to see color.

Contents

Introduction

My fascination with color began early on. My mother was an artist, and I spent hours watching her mix dabs of paint on her well-worn artist's palette. She painted and sketched hundreds of landscapes of Lake Harriet and areas in and around Minneapolis, each one completely different depending on the time of day and the season. The cool, blue-gray scenes she painted during the snowy, winter months made me feel sad and cold. I knew then that somehow I felt happier when the warm yellows and vibrant greens of spring appeared in her paintings. I realized at that young age that different colors can create different moods and that certain combinations of colors felt right while others didn't.

I studied my mother's art books and loved looking at the colors of the Impressionists, but especially loved the way the ancient Egyptians used color in their jewelry and on their furniture. From the dark, mysterious paintings of the Renaissance masters to the contemporaries like Alexander Kinsky, Picasso, and Cézanne, I fell in love with color, art, and design.

Though my artistic abilities may be limited, I was fortunate enough to inherit the creative ingredients from growing up in a home with an artist for a mother and an uncle and grandfather who were architects. It all resulted in my becoming an interior

designer. I've seen color trends come and go, furniture styles get reborn into the latest trendy designs, and home furnishing prices go sky-high, but one thing remains—color impacts our lives in many different ways, and it can create a home you feel proud of and welcome in.

If you're like most people, you probably feel like you don't know how to add color to your home. But don't shortchange yourself! Instead of leaving the decision up to your neighbor, or the salesman in the paint department at your local home center, take the information in this book and learn how to make good color choices. It may take some experimenting, but the end result, including the satisfaction of putting your mark on your home, will be well worth it.

Color Basics

Color makes the world a more beautiful place. Everything around us would be pretty boring if we only saw things in shades of gray. While we can't do much about the color that Mother Nature imparts on our world, we can use color to reflect our personality. In fact, color says a lot about who we are, whether those colors are conveyed through flowers we plant in a garden, the clothes we wear, or the furnishings in our home. Color can indicate whether a person is adventurous or conservative, and also communicate the feeling we want a room to convey—relaxing, energetic, fun, or whimsical.

Before you embark on redecorating any space in your home, it's important to first become aware of all the colors around you. To start, take note of the variety of colors you first already have in your home, even if your home appears to be all neutral. Don't focus only on the big things; look, too, at details and accents and you'll see a rainbow emerging. That being said, also look at your closet and accessories—we typically wear the colors we're most comfortable with. Once you've identified the colors you most love, think about how they make you and those around you feel. These colors and feelings are what you likely want to convey in your home.

Color is perhaps the most important element in interior design, but there are many things that influence the color we see, including light, pattern, texture, and the other colors that are nearby.

◀ FOR SOMEONE WHO likes a lot of color, a room like this is perfect, since it includes colors from the entire spectrum. This room works because no one color is overpowering. The rug—the inspiration for the room—ties the colors together.

The Effects of Light on Color

HUMAN VISION IS DEPENDENT on the presence of light. Together the eye and the brain distinguish the different wavelengths of radiant energy and translate light into color. The amount of light, as well as the kind of light, whether natural or artificial, will change how a color is perceived and ultimately what that color says about you and your home.

NATURAL LIGHT

Almost everyone has some natural light in their home. If you're lucky enough to have large windows and subsequently lots of natural light, you're seeing color at its best. The most evenly balanced light is daylight at midday. But daylight changes continuously, affecting the appearance of colors. Inside the home, where we usually have both natural and artificial light, absolute control of color is difficult, if not impossible.

Natural light also varies by geographical location, the weather, and the seasons. It also varies based on how your home is oriented on the land and where the sun is at certain times of the day. The light quality between Florida, New York, and Minnesota varies greatly. Shadows created by the mountains in Montana or Colorado also affect color inside the home. Even vegetation at different times of the year can have an impact on color. What this means is that selecting colors can be tricky, so it's important to be aware of how natural light and landscape conditions can influence your color choices, and to select the colors in the actual space where they will appear.

▶ A DRAMATIC LOOK usually requires either strong color or high contrast. This room contains both, from the saturated red-orange walls to the black furniture. The use of black in any room is an easy way to add drama.

▼ THIS GRACEFUL, curving wall is inviting because of the sunny wall color. The space takes advantage of both natural and artificial light to highlight the curve as well as the artwork.

▼ COLOR IS NOT CONSTANT. This all–white room will appear to change color many times during the day as the light and wall mirror create reflections and shadows.

ARTIFICIAL LIGHT ARTIFICIAL LIGHT

Artificial lighting is essential for comfort and convenience, and it can be used to accentuate and emphasize certain colors and architectural details, balance the color and light in the room, and even change the color and perceived size of objects.

Lightbulbs, too, have an impact on color in a room. In-candescent light is the most common type of artificial light in your home; while these bulbs typically cast a warm, soft glow, they lack colors from the blue end of the spectrum, so sometimes make a blue room look green.

Fluorescent light tends to enhance blues and greens, and today's bulbs have been improved to include the full color spectrum range. However, fluorescent light tends to dull reds, oranges, and yellows. Beware that many paint stores and home centers use fluorescent lighting, so use caution when selecting paint colors in these outlets.

Halogen bulbs, also known as quartz lamps, provide very clear, white light that is most similar to daylight. These bulbs enhance most color schemes. Just the opposite, candlelight— the warmest of all lights—enhances only reds, oranges, and yellows, and makes cool colors like blues and green dull.

COLOR SCHEMES THAT WORK

A large living room with lots of windows and high ceilings can have a cold feeling. But with the right colors and textures, large rooms can be inviting and warm.

INSPIRED BY the colors found in the fireplace, the walls in this living room are painted a soft gray, contrasting with the white painted trim. The white ceiling and beams add light and expand the space.

A FABRIC that ties a color scheme together is called a bridging fabric. The pillow fabric contains all the colors in the room and provides just enough of them to make the room feel cohesive. Bridging fabrics can also work well on a valance, bench, or chair seat cushion.

A WARM, red, gold and gray area rug contributes texture and keeps the room from looking bare.

A RIBBED fabric in a light, warm neutral on the chairs gives them a soft, inviting appearance.

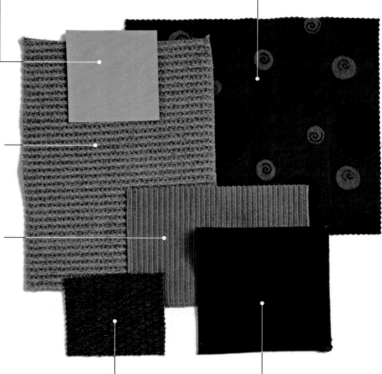

BECAUSE GRAY can feel cool, other warmer colors were added to the room. A textured olive green chenille fabric on the sofa brings in a natural feeling.

SOLID RED accent pillows in a fine texture draw color from the area rug for a burst of color throughout the room.

The Influence of Surfaces, Pattern, and Texture

WHEN SELECTING FABRICS and finishes for your home, it's important to realize that all materials have characteristics—texture and pattern—that modify the way color is seen. For example, a high-gloss finish on a wall tends to weaken all colors, making them appear lighter due to the reflected light. In addition, adjacent surfaces, such as a floor, reflecting that same wall can change a color's hue and tint the wall with its own color.

The texture of a surface can alter its perceived color due to tiny shadows at the microscopic level. Highly textured fabrics such as velvets, suedes, and chenille and pile may change color when observed at different angles because these textures absorb light, resulting in darker or lighter areas of color. Metallic surfaces, which are technically textured, reflect color in different ways. White metals that are polished, such as chrome, silver, and stainless steel, reflect colors like a mirror, changing color very little. But warm, polished metals such as brass, copper, and gold can tint colors with their own color. Tinted, colored mirrored walls also change the reflection of the room, often with confusing results.

Small-scale patterns on fabrics, rugs, or walls can change the overriding color of a room based on how the patterns are viewed. When viewed up close, small-scale, multicolored patterns separate the colors so that each color is distinct. But when viewed from a distance, the colors become mixed and the end result may be an unexpected and possibly unappealing third color. This third color is known as partitive color, or visual mix, and can be compared to the Impressionism and Pointillism painting techniques of using small dots of color, knowing that the eye will mix colors together and see them as a different color. In interior design, it's important to view small-scale multicolored patterns from a distance so that you have an accurate picture of the colors your room conveys.

▲ IF YOU'RE INTERESTED in updating an old color scheme, try a new wall color. But before investing in new upholstery or furniture, use throws or slipcovers over existing pieces to determine the colors and patterns you like best.

▲ EVEN THOUGH the gathered bed skirt is feminine, the black color and scale of the bed dominate the room, making it feel masculine. The yellow walls and red bedding are almost full intensity, reinforcing the strong statement.

◄ MOST PEOPLE CONSIDER white a noncolor, but in the paint industry, white is considered a tinted color. A high-quality paint, will produce the cleanest white. Comparing different whites will help you see how they differ. Here, crisp white walls make the wood and the furnishings stand out.

Deciphering the Color Wheel

MOST OF US ONLY REMEMBER the color wheel from high school art class, but even if you work with color on a daily basis, the color wheel can still be a mystery. Simply, the color wheel is an easy way of explaining the relationship of colors and why certain colors work together. By learning the vocabulary of color, you will be able to better understand how color works and use it to your advantage.

Interior design and any other situation where pigments (paint) and dyes (fabrics or yarns) are used involve the use of subtractive color. This is because any object or material (walls, floors, and furniture) absorbs or subtracts all the color except the color of the object, which is the color we see.

The basic color wheel consists of 12 colors—3 primary, 3 secondary, and 6 tertiary colors. There are an infinite number of gradations between colors. The colors that cannot be produced by mixing other colors are red, yellow, and blue, the three primary colors. Any other color can be made by mixing these colors together and adding white and black. When two adjacent primary colors are mixed together, they form the secondary color. For example, blue and yellow mixed together makes green. Orange and purple are the other secondary colors.

Between each of the primary and secondary colors are the tertiary colors. The tertiary colors are the hyphenated names that combine the two colors: Purple-red, red-orange, orange-yellow, yellow-green, green-blue, and blue-purple. Color names beyond the primary, secondary, and tertiary names are less precise and actually are confusing. Color names that refer to real objects—sand, leaf, bark, sky blue— are equally confusing because they are not specific.

▶ HAVE FUN WITH COLOR, even if it's only in your accents. Hot pink dining chairs, lime green placemats, and orange tulips and candles bring this plain wood tabletop to life.

▶ TO CREATE A BEDROOM that is restful and soothing, quiet colors should be used. These buttery yellow walls are complemented with a darker color ceiling to help visually lower the ceiling and make the room feel warm and more intimate.

◀ A SINGLE COLOR gives a room a straightforward, simple look. These deep chocolate brown walls are contrasted by painted white woodwork but are reinforced by the brown tones of the heavy wood table.

Color Attributes

THE COLOR SYSTEM developed by Albert Munsell is the most widely accepted in interior design today. In the Munsell system, color is described as having three attributes—hue, the name of the color family; value, the lightness or darkness of a color; and intensity (or chroma), the purity or saturation of a color.

COLOR FAMILIES

We refer to colors not only by their attributes but also by their family names, such as red or blue-green. We also tend to group colors in one of two groups: warm or cool. But any color can tend toward warm or cool. For example, red is considered a warm color, but a blue-based red is a cooler red than an orange-based red. For practical purposes, red, orange, and yellow are considered warm colors, and purple, blue, and green are considered cool colors. The color wheel is divided into these two families, which tend to spark emotional responses in people.

Warm Colors

Warm colors tend to advance, or move toward you. Included in the warm category are reds, oranges, and yellows, as well as the tints, tones, and shades of the warm colors—pinks, peaches, coral, coppers, golds, browns, and burgundy. Warm color schemes work well in large rooms because they create a cozy feeling. A warm color painted on a high ceiling can make it seem lower. And rooms that don't have a lot of light can benefit from walls painted in a sunny, warm yellow. The deepest warm colors, like brown and burgundy, seem to raise the room temperature, so work well in intimate settings. In rooms where the dominant colors are warm, cool colors work well as accents.

Cool Colors

Cool colors tend to recede, or move away from you. Cool colors work well in climates that are very warm. Many cool colors can take on warm characteristics if the tint or shade

▲ TRANSLUCENT, COLORED STAINS, like the red on the paneling shown here, retain the natural look of wood while adding color. Stained paneling allows the knots and grain of the wood to show through, adding texture as well.

THE GEOMETRIC SHAPES of these furnishings are enhanced by their strong materials and colors, including the slatted coffee table, dark painting, and steel fan. The room is anchored by the black rug, which also brings in texture and pattern.

of the color is on the warm side. For instance, blue can be very soothing when it's a bit green—think of the Caribbean Ocean—or icy when it's more silvery. Accents in warm colors help a room from feeling too cool.

Neutral colors

Neutrals are colors of low chroma that don't appear to belong in any one color family (even though they do). Gray, black, taupe, white, tan, and beige are all considered neutrals even though they all contain color. Neutrals can be warm or cool depending on what they are combined with. Combining neutrals successfully is a difficult thing to do because they can contain hints of pink, green, purple, or other colors. Even an all-white scheme will contain a range of varying whites that can appear different based on the sheen, texture, pattern, and light.

GRAY STONE AND BLUE-GRAY walls would seem chilly without the light-colored trim and ceiling to help warm things up. Lots of natural light as well as the light from the three ceiling fixtures offset the effects of the cool colors.

Color and Mood

OUR LIFELONG EXPERIENCES, associations, and cultural interactions affect how we react to color. Generally, most of us will react in a similar way to the same colors, but certain memories can cause you to love, or strongly dislike, a particular color.

It is wellknown that certain colors are associated with certain moods. Red and orange, for example, stimulate the appetite and increase energy. Green is associated with calm, growth, and openness; yellow with sunlight and optimism. But within each color family are extremes that can't necessarily be interpreted with the same kind of emotion and mood. The reaction to a harsh, acid green is completely different than to a warm, natural shade of green. A bright, lemony yellow gives a very different feeling than a soft, buttery yellow. A highly saturated blue-red can be disturbing in large amounts and possibly increase anger, but a toned-down version of a rosy-red can have a calming effect.

▲ STAINED GLASS is an effective way to add color subtly, particularly when the sun is shining on it. This custom skylight mimics nature, making visitors feel as though they're still outdoors even when they're not.

◄ THIS SLEEP-INDUCING, monochromatic scheme uses a variety of blues plus cream for a relaxing effect. The creamy bedcover, painted trim, and window sheers provide subtle contrast while supporting the intended feeling.

The Emotions of Color

Full-strength colors can cause very different emotional reactions than tints or shades of the same colors. Before determining which colors you want in a room, spread out a variety of paint chips (the larger, the better). You may find that by adjusting colors slightly you'll get the emotional reaction you want.

- Too much red can be irritating, but soft pink is calming.
- Blue and violet are calming, but a room with too much blue can make a person look ill.
- Deep orange adds excitement, but bright orange can look cheap.
- Deep purple imparts loneliness, but soft violet is subduing.
- Brown can be associated with melancholy or stability when the shade is earthy.
- White imparts purity and brightness of spirit, but a blue-white can look sterile.
- Yellow is cheerful and healthful but also means caution.
- Black can be empty and depressing but used in the right way can be dramatic as well.

▼ COLOR CAN BE USED in a porch to bring the outside in or to carry an interior color scheme out. This transitional area is connected to both the indoors and out thanks to the dominant green color on the trim and furniture and natural stone floor.

COLOR SCHEMES THAT WORK

Not quite pastels, these mid-value colors are repeated from room to room, connecting the two with color. Because the colors are of similar strength, the rooms feel well balanced.

THE SOFA COLOR in the living areas mirrors that of the area rug in the dining room, tying the two rooms together. Likewise, the beam that divides the two areas is painted the same color, acting as a bridge between the rooms.

THE SUNNY yellow drapery fabric repeats the color of the walls and brings sunshine into the room.

A PILLOW fabric similar to the colors used on the dining chairs adds a small bit of pattern to these plain surfaces.

GREEN, PINK, AND YELLOW paint colors repeat and balance the fabric colors, and are contrasted by pure-white wood base moldings and light wood floors.

Adding Color to Your Home

Choosing color for your home can be overwhelming, especially when facing rows of hundreds of paint chips or bolts of fabric. Before you even start to think about building a color scheme, look first at what colors are in your home now. Do these colors work for you and create the emotion you're looking for (relaxing, energetic, playful)? If you aren't surrounded by colors that make you feel good then you need to change them. Color is personal, so the first step is to think about where you find inspiration.

One of the best places to get ideas for your color scheme is to walk through furniture stores. The better retail stores and design studios know how to use color and what colors work best together. They are also up to the minute on the trends and can provide you with the items you'll need to complete the design of your room. You'll not only gather ideas for colors, but also for style and accessories.

After you've chosen your colors, try them out in the space before making a commitment. A 2-in. sample may appeal to you when you're in the store, but that same color in your home may look all wrong. Don't be shy about asking your retailer for large samples to take home.

◄ NEUTRAL WALLS AND UPHOLSTERY put emphasis on a room's artwork and decorative objects. The black table helps to balance the strength of the painting with the light surfaces in this dining room.

Finding Inspiration

INSPIRATION CAN COME from anywhere, from your last vacation at the shore to the changing color of a maple leaf to your latest hair color. Mother Nature is the best decorator—she paints the world with every possible color and combination—and can be a wonderful source of inspiration. Here are some other ideas for finding what makes you the most happy:

- Go for a walk. Notice the subtle variations in the earth and plants, the dramatic colors of black and yellow on a bumblebee, the soft neutrals of sand and shells on the beach.

- Open your closet door. The colors you like to wear are those you feel comfortable with.

- Go to an art gallery or museum. Find a painting that really appeals to you and note the colors you see.

- Look around your house for a treasured collection. What colors are dominant?

- Check out the cover of food magazines. What's on the plate? Research has found that the more color there is on the plate the more likely the magazine will get picked up off the shelf.

- Flip through your favorite magazines and books. Look for photos in articles and advertisements that speak to you.

- Watch a movie. Pay close attention to the backgrounds; they might provide you with an idea for your home.

▲ SOFT, PALE SHADES of pink and cream are the perfect combination for a lady's bedroom. White painted furniture and white walls show off the pink fabrics. If this room had dark stained trim or furniture, the effect would not be as pleasing or as fresh looking.

▶ COLOR CAN BE USED to enhance the natural feeling you want to get from a room. The palette of greens and yellows, inspired by the floral rug as well as Mother Nature, makes this sunroom feel like spring and summer year-round.

Did You Know...

A small, expanding file is a great way to start a color idea file; it can hold paint chips, magazine clippings, and fabric swatches. Over time you'll begin to see a pattern forming in what you like. It can also help you discover your decorating style.

▲ MAINLY COMPRISED OF WOOD and stone, the rustic character is confirmed by the use of all-natural materials in this lodge-style bedroom. Since most of the permanent surfaces fall into the "neutral" category, the bedding could have been almost any color. The classic, traditional colors of burgundy and forest green in the quilt are reminiscent of a turn-of-the-century cabin.

◄ NOT FOR THE TIMID, this orange and yellow dining room is loaded with heat. The intense orange is limited to one accent wall and relieved by the use of a lighter, softer color on the adjacent wall. If both walls had been painted orange, the room might be overwhelming. The hot colors are balanced by the blue accents in the art and on the table.

COLOR SCHEMES THAT WORK

There's no need to limit your color choices to ones you've used in the past or those that seem "safe." This bedroom envelops the room with the warm melon color, which is even used on the ceiling, but doesn't feel too hot thanks to the unexpected use of purple-blue accents and the smooth, cool floor tile.

THE RED, orange, and yellow silk drapery fabric (which is also used as a table square) contains the largest amount of pattern in this bedroom. The smooth, iridescent silk naturally reflects light.

THE SOLID GOLDEN yellow underskirt has a slight texture that complements the smoothness of the plaid drapes and table square.

THE WALL COLOR and ceiling color is based on one of the colors in the plaid drapery fabric. When the ceiling color is the same as the wall it wraps a room, giving it a cocoon effect.

YELLOW'S complementary color, purple, is a smart choice in this room because the color offers a spot of relief from the oranges and yellows, and the quilted fabric provides contrast to the larger geometric drapes and table covering.

THE BRIGHT orange accent pillow keeps the heat throughout the room but brings in texture as well.

THE BEDDING, headboard, and bed skirt add relief to the colorful scheme thanks to their neutral color and smooth texture.

FOR TWO OF THE pillow shams, a traditional damask fabric adds another pattern to the room while maintaining the color scheme and adding elegance.

Taking Inventory

FEW DECORATING PROJECTS start from scratch, where the color possibilities are unlimited. So the next step in formulating your color plan is to look at the "givens"—the existing things in your home you need to work with, such as furniture or carpet, the color of a brick or stone fireplace, countertops, tile, or draperies. It's important to pay attention to the givens when choosing colors for a room, even if you don't like the color you're being forced to work with. (There are ways to downplay that color.) Take an inventory of everything including what these things are, their color, and the role they play in the room (major piece or accent). Create a small file of samples of these items (paint chips, fabric swatches, carpet, etc.) that you can keep with you when shopping for other elements in the room. If you don't have samples of those items, try to match the colors to paint chips for reference—it's difficult to "remember" color when you're not a home.

Be observant, since many items that look like just one color are actually made up of multiple colors in their patterns or textures and can also be affected by light. Granite countertops, for instance, often are made up of a dominant color and flecks of other colors. Likewise, a carpet might take on a brown tone when brushed in one direction but more red when brushed in the other. If elements like these will remain in your home, consider making them the inspiration for your color scheme.

▲ IN THE KITCHEN, a black-and-white color scheme could be austere. But here it takes on a warm, contemporary feel thanks to the yellow walls, pitched ceiling, and unique glass block window. White cabinetry keeps the focus on the window and ceiling.

▶ EVEN IN ALL-NEUTRAL homes, a little color is needed. In this remodeled kitchen, the color comes from blue glass pendant fixtures and two glass bowls, which is just enough with the rich wood tones. Accents like these are easy to change when the urge arises.

◀ LIKE OPENING A BOX of crayons, the colors in this family room form a palette that's youthful, creating the perfect backdrop for a family to play and relax together.

▲ IF YOU'RE NOT COMFORTABLE with colored bathroom fixtures, use the standard white and provide color in the walls and accents, which are easy to change.

Creating a Color Scheme

A COLOR SCHEME IS A SET of colors that creates a pleasing look. The best ones use a minimum of two or three colors but no more than six since the more colors you use, the more difficult it is to achieve a cohesive look. You probably already have at least one color you like; pick two more and then expand on that. Try using different values of each color; for example, light green and dark green, or pink and red. The most important thing to remember is that all colors need to be viewed in relationship to those near them in order to create a scheme that holds together.

There are five basic types of color schemes—monochromatic, complementary, analogous, split complementary, and triadic. The simplest to understand and the easiest to create is a **monochromatic** scheme. It is based on variations of tints and shades of one color family. For example, a monochromatic room could consist of colors from the brown family—a deep brown carpet, beige upholstery, and off-white draperies. A monotone scheme, different from a monochromatic scheme, uses one color but doesn't vary the tints and shades and ends up creating a room that looks boring.

A **complementary** scheme uses colors that are directly opposite each other on the color wheel. A complementary

▲ AN EASY WAY to reinforce a color scheme is by painting the interior of a bookcase, cabinet, or hutch in a color you want to emphasize. The green bookcase here not only does that but also makes the blue-and-white china collection stand out.

Basic Types of Color Schemes

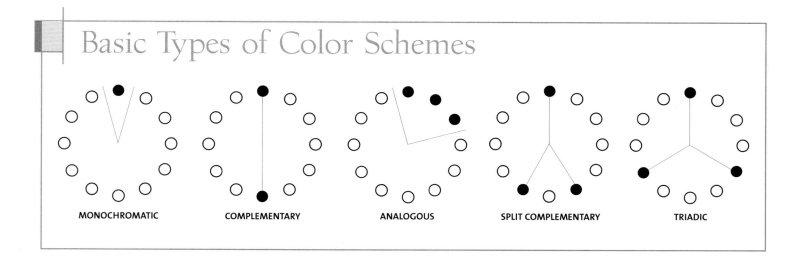

MONOCHROMATIC   COMPLEMENTARY   ANALOGOUS   SPLIT COMPLEMENTARY   TRIADIC

● ● ● ●

◀ SOPHISTICATION is created by the use of black columns and furniture combined with shocking orange accents. The high drama of these dominant colors requires that the largest backgrounds, the walls and floors, be kept neutral.

▼ GRAY, A COLOR that's usually cool, is balanced here by the warm, soft yellow walls, draperies, and pillows. Inspired by the colors found in the patterned rug, the color scheme even includes creamy white, in the headboard, to unify the room.

scheme works best when the colors used are not the same intensity; for example, pale pink combined with bright green where the pink is the main color and the green is an accent.

When colors that are adjacent to each other on the color wheel are combined in a room, an **analogous** color scheme is created. Generally any analogous color scheme works because the colors share similar characteristics.

A **split complementary** color scheme is created when colors that lie on both sides of a color's complement are combined. An example of this is a room that uses purple, yellow-green, and yellow-orange. To pull off this type of scheme, start with a pattern that contains all the colors you want to work with.

A **triadic** scheme, similar to a split complementary scheme, uses any three hues on the color wheel located equidistant from one another, such as red, yellow, and blue.

COLOR SCHEMES THAT WORK

Taken from the warm side of the color wheel this analogous scheme bursts with color. Orange, yellow-green, lime, and raspberry form a scheme that uses white to make the colors stand out. The walls could have been painted any one of these bright colors, but the room would have conveyed a completely different feeling.

AN EFFECTIVE treatment of using the same pattern in two different ways, the orange floral pillows match the rug but on a smaller scale.

GREEN, usually considered a cool color, is warm here because it contains so much yellow. Since it's used on multiple surfaces—pillows and wicker—it helps to tie the space together.

A LIME GREEN plaid adds a burst of color as an accent pillow.

BALANCING THE whole room is the bright pink distributed throughout in the cushions. Because this color has a darker look compared to the other colors, it provides more visual weight. If it had not been used on the sofa pillows, the room may have seemed off-balance.

SIMILAR TO THESE colors, the rug in the photo was most likely the element that inspired the room's colors. The orange background makes the room welcoming.

Linking Rooms with Color

ALTHOUGH ROOMS CAN FEEL separate from each other based on the number and size of doorways, don't think of them as individual spaces. It's important to create a unified flow of color from one space to the next to create a harmonious feel throughout your home. This doesn't mean that all rooms need to be the same colors; what works as a dominant color in one room can function as an accent in the next. Try using a thread of one color in each room to create a cohesive feeling, but to add variety, change the value of the color, adding intensity and interest or keeping it subdued and tinted.

If your home has an open floor plan, limit the number of abrupt color changes in order to move the eye seamlessly throughout the space. And if your home is small, it helps to make all the walls a similar color so that fewer boundaries are created. Your flooring can help expand space as well. Use the same color carpeting throughout. Or, if you need to change between tile, wood, and carpet, keep the basic tones similar. Since any contrast between light and dark will emphasize boundaries.

Don't forget about trim and architectural elements. Both of these can be highlighted with color or downplayed to diminish their prominence. When the color of wall and window trim and flooring are consistent from room to room, the spaces will be more unified than if the colors were different. You might even decide to keep the trim and the fireplace mantel the same color as the walls as a way to blend them into the whole space.

Keep in mind that color can create some surprising effects. Light colors will appear lighter against a dark background, and dark colors will seem darker against a light background. A mid-value color can be made to seem lighter or darker, depending on the background. And a neutral color may appear warm against a blue background but cool against a red background.

▲ REPETITION OF COLOR is key when your home has an open floor plan and you can see from one room to the next. The red color on the two chairs by the fireplace is carried through to the walls of the adjacent room. Without the red wall color to connect the spaces, the chairs would look out of place.

◀ THIS SUCCESSFUL analogous color scheme combines blue and green from the cool side of the spectrum. The two-story-high ceiling is emphasized by the tall drapery panels, which call attention to the windows while strengthening the color scheme.

▼ IN SPACES WHERE there's little opportunity to introduce a lot of color, bright touches can add pizzazz. The yellow wall color in the powder room and the bright green in the stairway were pulled out of the stained-glass window, bringing life to the wood tones that dominate the whole space.

COLOR SCHEMES THAT WORK

A white-on-white room can be highly sophisticated or just plain boring. The trick is to have subtle tonal variations and a variety of patterns and textures, as demonstrated here.

A THROW IN CHENILLE helps interrupt all the smooth surfaces and adds a cozy look. This "white" is a slightly different tone. When using white, don't get too concerned with matching exact shades and tints; the variation can be pleasing.

AN IMPORTANT element to creating a successful all-white room like this is to have a little contrast for tension. The painted, worn white finish on the vanity table works to keep the look light while the dark chair finish provides the contrast.

DECORATIVE TRIM on pillows and window treatments can add texture and detail. This trim combines white with taupe for added variety.

A MATELASSE FABRIC, normally used as a bedcover, can be used to upholster a chaise or chair. This classic, one-color version has the fabric's typical small pattern. Because of the quilted effect, the fabric contributes subtle pattern and texture to the room.

A SLIGHT VARIATION between the trim color and the wall color adds depth to any room. Here, slightly more creamy colors were used to add a warmer tone to the room. If a stark white wall color had been used, the room could have felt cold.

A GAUZY, white fabric forms graceful swags and softly frames the window. The sheerness of the fabric allows light to pass through.

THIS SMOOTH, white fabric, used in smaller amounts on the bench and chair cushions, has a subtle geometric design that complements the curvy shapes of the matelasse fabric. In a monochromatic room like this, it's important to vary the patterns to keep things interesting.

Green

ost homes contain a touch of green somewhere, even if just a green plant. It's the color people associate most with nature and is as varied as nature itself. From deep, dark, forest greens to bright yellow-greens, most shades of green work well inside the home because almost any other color goes with green.

Green is the color of balance and harmony; in fact, it's right in the middle in the color spectrum. Usually referred to as a cool color, a true mid-green is neither warm nor cool. But a green-blue easily takes on a cool, watery feeling; just the opposite, green-yellow can become warm and earthy.

So what does this mean for your home? If you're attracted to green and considering using it for a room, think about how you want the room to feel. What is the room used for? Is it a room where you want a calming feeling or where you need energy? Is it a room where you want to feel cool or warm? Look at all the varieties of green— from classic to earthy, bright to sophisticated and fresh—and think about how they make you feel. Certain shades of green may remind you of your grandmother's house, while other greens look current and youthful. Then, think about which colors go with the green you like.

◄ WITH THE FURNISHINGS and carpet mainly neutral, the wall color in this bedroom could have been any color. The use of green helps to keep the eye moving beyond the walls and to the outside, through the large windows. The view would not have been as much of a focal point if the walls had been a bright red, for instance.

Greens

Green is the color of rejuvenation, new plants, optimism, and youth. It is also known to reduce blood pressure and can help us feel balanced. Lighter, toned greens are relaxing and restful, especially when combined with warm peach or rose tones, while deeper greens are sophisticated and intimate.

▲ WALLS AND WINDOW trim painted in the same grass green make the furnishings stand out. The neutral chair was needed for visual relief from all the color.

▼ GREEN AND BROWN is a natural combination because the two commonly occur together in nature. They give this contemporary bedroom an earthy feel, with the leaf green walls, wood armoire, and bed linens.

Color on Cabinetry

Don't overlook your cabinetry as a place to use color. Unexpected combinations can add pizzazz to your kitchen or bathroom. And be creative in the use: Consider a different color on an island than on the perimeter cabinets, or paint the doors a different color than the cabinet box. If you're thinking of using colored cabinetry, first consider your countertops, since their color and pattern will help inform what color you use on the cabinets.

▲ THE YELLOW COUNTER and light-colored wood floor brighten this traditional kitchen, which gets its color from classic green cabinets. Yellow and red accents punctuate the space so that the green isn't too overpowering.

◄ THE LIME-GREEN CABINETRY reflects the daring personality of the homeowner, but she smartly chose to restrict the amount of the color. The natural wood island and white countertop and backsplash add welcome relief and give the room a fresh look.

Classic

THE CLASSIC COLORS in the green family are those that seem more traditional than modern. These are the greens that have been established over time, not trendy or dated. They can be deep greens, like forest green and hunter green, or lighter gray-greens like moss green or olive green. They can even be pale, toned greens.

The classic shades are "safe," providing color without it screaming at you. Use two to three different values of classic shades for subtle effects. Or use a classic green with contrasting colors like red or orange for a more dramatic look. Whichever classic green you choose, you can be assured it will stand the test of time.

▲ THE TONED-DOWN HUE of this green sofa could have made this room feel dark if the color palette were different. Here the neutral walls add brightness, and the red in the pillows and accents add strength and variety.

◄ DEEP FOREST GREEN walls give this living room a stately and dignified look. The window trim, wainscoting, and carpet are all kept light, allowing for the dark green to add drama throughout the room by repeating in the sofa. Red and gold are natural accents to this shade of green.

Did You Know...

Reflective surfaces help to keep dark walls from appearing too dark and make them less dominant. For this reason, hang mirrors, artwork, and other accessories that have some reflective properties on a dark wall.

▲ THE OUTSIDE IS BROUGHT into this breakfast room because of the soft, natural green trim, which makes the divided-glass windows and doors seem less of a barrier to the outside; instead, they blend with the foliage outside.

Earthy

BECAUSE OF GREEN'S strong tie to nature, many shades fall into the "earthy" category—this feeling of back to nature and letting the outside in. In fact, many of the words used to describe green—moss, avocado, fir, celery—are derived from nature. We tend to think of earthy greens as those that are a bit more "dirty" than clear. Earthy greens have some of the same characteristics as the classic greens, and they can work well in traditional and transitional settings. Wood finishes, complementary colors, and neutrals reinforce the elements of the outdoors. Beige-toned neutrals can be used, to terra-cotta and clay colors, and browns of all kinds work well with earthy greens.

▲ A GREEN FLORAL fabric combines the neutral colors from the stone fireplace as well as the wood tones, bringing together all the colors of the room.

◄ IF YOU'RE LUCKY enough to have high ceilings, take the opportunity to try a deep shade of your favorite green. Here, the light-colored beamed ceiling enhances the tropical green walls and keeps the room from feeling closed in.

► CONSIDER ALL SURFACES in a space when choosing colors. Cherry woodwork in this Craftsman-style home is highlighted by the use of a warm, earthy gray-green color as an accent on some of the walls and the slate floor. The flooring pulls together the dominant colors—green and coppery red.

COLOR SCHEMES THAT WORK

When a room's color scheme consists of mainly one color, texture takes on extra importance as a way to provide interest and create a mood. Natural fibers add a casual, informal feeling to a room whereas glass sculpture and painted canvases both provide a more contemporary, cool feeling.

A SOLID GREEN FABRIC on the chair provides relief from all the pattern and texture in the room.

ACCENT PILLOWS that combine the green and a complementary warm color keep the colors balanced in the room.

A SMOOTH neutral fabric makes for a pleasing contrast with the heavily textured frame of the sofa and allows opportunity to use patterned pillows.

AN UNEXPECTED brush fringe adds character.

PLAID PILLOW CUSHIONS unify all the colors of the room including the oriental rug.

SOFT GREEN WALLS are emphasized by the painted wood trim. The wood chair frames, also painted, repeat the trim color.

A WOVEN SEA GRASS SOFA contributes texture and a natural element.

Bright

BRIGHT GREENS are those that can be a bit shocking and daring, like lime-yellow and intense grass green. Used alone or in combination with other equally strong colors, bright greens create a sense of high energy. It's usually wise to combine these shades of green with neutrals like black or white—the neutrals not only provide relief to the eye but also show off the color. If you're not prepared to use a bright green on a wall or as the main color in a room, use it as an accent color to provide visual punch; bright green accents are also an effective way to update a traditional setting.

▲ TRADITIONAL CABINETRY STYLE meets contemporary color in this library. The area rug was the likely inspiration for both the cabinet and wall colors. The crisp, white trim provides necessary visual relief.

◄ ONLY A SMALL AMOUNT of bright, Granny Smith Apple—green is all that's needed in this kitchen to bring the room to life. The color was repeated in the hallway to unify the two areas. The abundance of white woodwork makes the green stand out.

◄ SOMETIMES THE COLOR
in a room provides dominance, and sometimes the style of the furnishings do. Here both do their share. This color combination is unique and adds bits of shocking color to the room. The sleek and modern furnishings are neutral, allowing their form to stand out.

▲ GETTING CREATIVE WITH COLOR
is one way to get attention. Bright green, yellow, and white make this stairway playful and fun. Painting the stair risers in a bright color is not only creative, but also makes the stairs easier to see.

COLOR SCHEMES THAT WORK

Using the same trim color throughout a space that doesn't have an obvious color scheme can help bring consistency to a room. A light trim color almost requires that something else in the room be of a similar light tone, even if it's just a lamp shade. When combined with soft, pale colors, white trim can have a subtle and soothing effect. But when combined with bright or deep colors, white trim makes the colors stand out and appear more intense.

A FRESH GREEN WALL COLOR is accented by crisp white wood trim, giving the room an up to date burst of color. The walls could have been painted red, white, or even black, but each would have made the room feel completely different.

A WHITE LINEN slipcover on the sofa keeps the room looking fresh. The large dose of white was needed to keep the eye moving around the room.

RED, THE ACCENT COLOR chosen for the pillow, was inspired by the red in the rug. If the red pillow were not added, the rug would look disconnected from the rest of the space.

A BLACK AND WHITE houndstooth gives this 50s-style Danish chair a surprising new look and helps to connect the other dark elements in the room.

Subtle and Sophisticated

SUBTLE AND SOPHISTICATED green schemes give a room a quiet, calm feeling. These schemes usually consist of one or two shades of green that allow the elements of the room—not the color—to take center stage. If you really want your furnishings to stand out, use a mono-chromatic scheme where the green is soft and toned or use a few green accents in an all-neutral room.

▲ CREATE A CALMING atmosphere by pairing only one soft color with white. This is the perfect effect in a bedroom that functions as a retreat, since the color scheme is subtle and doesn't demand its own attention. If the bedroom is for a teenager, consider vibrant colors that provide energy and contrast.

◄ A TWO-COLOR SCHEME like this one is easy to create and is guaranteed to work. Start by using analogous colors to give the space harmony, as was done in this bedroom of pale green and yellow.

Did You Know...

If you're searching for inspiration for a color scheme, rely on one of the main elements of a room, such as countertops or cabinetry in a bathroom, which can be a particularly challenging space. Then repeat the colors of that element elsewhere in the room to help tie the space together.

▲ BECAUSE EVERYTHING ELSE in this room is neutral, the green stands out even though it's used just on accent pieces. A room with this type of color scheme—neutral background with colored accents—is very flexible, and can be updated quickly and inexpensively.

Fresh

FRESH GREENS are shades that have been tinted with white, so the final result is a clean look, not toned down or drab. These greens range from pale to mid-value shades and work well in any decorating style because they give the feeling of optimism. You can hardly go wrong with shades of these greens, whether you want to introduce lots of color in a room or simply sprinkle it in through the accessories, such as lamp shades or window treatments, because they are gender-neutral. This makes them especially appropriate for a nursery, bedroom, or living room. And because they go well with other fresh shades of pink, yellow, and blue, finding colors to accent with is a breeze.

▲ GREEN IS GENDER-FRIENDLY and timeless, making it a practical color in a nursery or young child's bedroom. Accents in any color, from pink or light blue to orange, brown, or violet, will let you customize the look for your child.

◄ A BOLD, DEEP BLUE pillow acts like an exclamation point, giving the room a pop of color and keeping it from looking all too much the same value in this predominantly green and yellow bedroom.

▶ A LIGHT, CLEAN VALUE of green on the walls gives this room a fresh look, especially when combined with white woodwork. The wall color, repeated in the floral area rug, reinforces the color scheme in the furniture fabric. Pink, not red, was chosen for the accent color here for a lighter hand and a feminine look.

ANDRÉ DERAIN: LANDSCAPE IN SOUTHERN FRANCE
Museum of Fine Arts, Boston

Blue

oted as the favorite color in America, blue's popularity is undeniable. Blue is a color that can easily be warm or cool in its own right, and it certainly takes on aspects of either based on its hue and tone as well as the other colors paired with it.

In the 1870s, colored-light therapy to cure physical and emotional conditions was the rage. Pseudo-scientists prescribed blue light to help treat nervous conditions and control inflammations, headaches, and sunstroke, among other things. While blue will likely not cure what ails you, it does affect most people in the same way. That is, it is soothing and calming, and brings out our deepest emotions, typically those that make us happy and friendly.

Blue is most often associated with water, so it is typically found in homes that are near water or in climates where a cool feeling is desired. When used in large amounts, blue can create a cold environment, though, so it's often used in combination with warm colors to help create balance. Earthy browns, oranges, yellows, and reds of all kinds pair nicely with blues because they come from the opposite end of the color spectrum.

CONSIDER YOUR STONE and tile colors when choosing wall color. The slate tile in this bathroom has varied blues, grays, and other natural colors within it, making the deep blue wall color a good choice. Even the reddish color of the vanity cabinet relates to the colors in the floor, giving this room a cohesive feeling.

◄ NAVY BLUE WALLS can make a room feel warm, especially when combined with complementary colors, like the reds and pinks in this living room. Because the blue is so dark, it doesn't feel cold. In addition, the blue is contrasted with the white woodwork, making the walls stand out more than if the woodwork had been stained dark.

▼ THE AMOUNT OF COLOR a person can tolerate varies greatly. In this bedroom, blue is everywhere but gets a little relief from the white bed linens and white furniture.

◀ REPETITION—OF COLOR AND SHAPES—is the key here. The pale blue wall color repeats the color in the prints and the chair seat. In addition, the prints are all framed in the same molding and contain the same kind of images, giving the room rhythm.

▼ HAVE YOU EVER noticed how some colors naturally go well with certain wood tones? The warm, reddish-brown tone of the woodwork in this bedroom and exercise room seems to demand a cool blue color with it.

MOODMAKERS

Blues

Many believe that blue is a de-stresser. When used in combination with warm colors, it can stimulate creativity and nurturing. Deep indigo blue, nearly black, has been found to induce sleep and bring out our deepest emotions. Loyalty, honesty, and integrity are related to the saturated blues, such as royal blue.

Classic

LIKE A FAVORITE pair of worn blue jeans, classic blue is a staple in many homes. It speaks to tradition, timelessness, and comfort. But classic blue is no longer just navy or French country. Variations of these hues have expanded the range, making the tried-and-true more up to date. Think about classic blue in terms of denim jeans. While the old standby straight-up denim is still available, stone-washed, acid-washed, and ripped versions have added texture, pattern, and color variation that people of all ages have come to like.

And so it is the same for your home. If your style is traditional English or French, then blue is the perfect color for you. But because, like other classics, it never goes out of style, it mixes well with many other colors, from bright to subtle. Many fabrics used with these traditional styles have blue in them, providing a starting point for a color scheme.

▲ CLASSIC BLUE WALLS in an all-white bathroom is a timeless look that's never out of style. This bold, monochromatic scheme is bright and inviting that will withstand the test of time.

RUSTIC, WOODEN ACCENTS and beams clearly add to the classic character of this room, but the real focal point is the blue armoire, which provides color and emphasis. The same blue is found in the pattern of the rug and again in the artwork.

PAINTED OR STAINED cabinets add color and warmth to a kitchen. The traditional style of these cabinets is enhanced by the color, which is repeated in the rug. Painting or staining old cabinets is a good way to bring them alive while providing color at the same time.

Did You Know...

When selecting finishes for a room, it's OK to have painted as well as stained woodwork. In most cases, though, it's wise to limit your wood finishes to no more than two or three.

▲ INTERESTING CEILING LINES become more prominent when they're painted a color other than white. The blue color of this ceiling is repeated in the pillows, tying the spaces together and making the space feel intimate.

Did You Know...

The easiest way to give a neutral bathroom a little pizzazz is to include color from the adjacent room. Add color to the walls or ceiling, or bring it in with towels, rugs, soaps, and other decorative items.

▷ EVEN A SINK and soap dish can provide welcome personality to an otherwise neutral bathroom.

◁ IT'S WISE TO CONSIDER the tone of the floor and colors in the rug when choosing wall color. Because the floor here is warm and light, it allows the opportunity to use strong color on the walls. The blue walls actually make the china stand out and give the room a sense of intimacy.

COLOR SCHEMES THAT WORK

This complementary color scheme uses blue for the dominant color and keeps the room focused on the nautical nature so that it doesn't detract from the view. White woodwork, draperies, and walls add a fresh quality to the scene.

PLAIN, WHITE LINEN draperies keep the focus on the view out the windows. If the draperies had been done in the striped fabric or any kind of pattern, your eye would have stopped at the window. Simple window treatments are best on any window where the view is the emphasis.

PLAIDS AND STRIPES can work together, provided the colors harmonize and the scale of the patterns vary.

ADDING ANOTHER shade of blue keeps the palette from looking too much the same. This fabric has a little texture, reminiscent of the canvas used for sails.

BOLD PATTERNS like the blue-and-white stripe on the sofa need to be balanced in a room. By placing pillows in the same stripe on the solid sofa, your eye continues to move throughout the room by attracting your attention without overwhelming it.

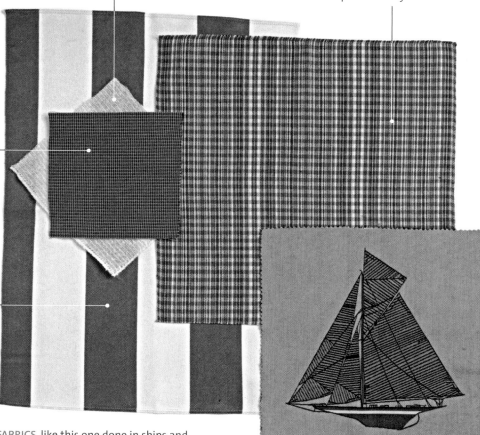

FUN FABRICS, like this one done in ships and lighthouses, can add lots of personality to a room. These kinds of "theme" fabrics are best used in small amounts combined with solids and geometrics.

Bold and Bright

THESE BLUES seem to pop and have a life of their own. The blues that fall into this category are typically bright and highly saturated, not muddied or toned. Bright royal blue, aqua, and turquoise are examples of these energetic blues and work well either alone or when paired with equally bright colors like red, coral, and yellow. It's not so much the blues by themselves but rather the colors they are used with that give a room dramatic appeal. Paired with brown, they're sophisticated. Teamed with red or orange, they're lively, and with pale pink, they're easy on the eyes.

Consider using bold blues in rooms where there's lots of activity and movement because they are stimulating, especially when combined with other brights. These are good blues to use in exercise rooms but not good to use in large amounts in kitchens.

▲ A SENSE OF PLAYFULNESS is evident in this dining room that uses primary colors to grab attention. The navy blue stair wall is used as a backdrop to emphasize the unusual multicolored stair railing that repeats all the colors in the room. If that wall had been painted a lighter color, the railing would not be as apparent.

◄ TROPICAL COLORS COMBINE to create a happy, carefree look for this built-in bookcase. The stairs make a perfect spot for reading a book or dreaming about lounging on the beach of the Caribbean.

TURQUOISE IS A GOOD CHOICE to use in a warm climate or anywhere you want to be reminded of one. With the floor tile reminiscent of the floor of a swimming pool and the walls and ceiling representing the sky, this kitchen makes after-dinner cleanup less of a chore. Even the color of the cabinet knobs seems like a splash of water.

CEILINGS DON'T NEED to be white. This one is painted a sky blue that actually makes the ceiling seem higher. A deeper blue bed covering balances the room and visually helps to "push" the ceiling higher.

▲ INTENSE BLUE AND RED create a color scheme that's bold and vibrant. The dramatic, deep blue walls contrast with the adjacent neutral walls, emphasizing the sitting alcove and architectural detail. The red adds energy while the deep blue provides a bit of a calming effect.

Did You Know...

In a room that's mainly one color, accents in its opposite color will counteract the color and add interest. If the room is mainly in warm tones, add a cool accent. If the room is mainly in cool colors, add a warm accent.

▲ WHILE A BLUE LIKE THIS might be too strong for other kinds of rooms, teamed with white woodwork and cabinets, it gives the laundry room a fresh, clean look.

◄ WARM, GOLDEN PINE wood flooring helps to keep this bathroom from looking cold. A deep blue lacquer on the vanity cabinet and door trim is carried through to the adjoining room as an accent color in the tiles. The light blue walls, white countertop, and chrome fixtures keep things fresh.

Soothing and Peaceful

TINTED, SOFT BLUES like Robin's egg, sky, and blue-gray are examples of tranquil, peaceful blues. Toned down with gray or tinted with green, these blues range from light to mid-value and combine well with complementary colors like peach or salmon. Small amounts of brighter accent colors, like orange or bright pink, can work well with these pales, as long as the accents don't overtake the blue background.

These blues can lean toward green, making it hard to tell if they are green or blue. When the blues tend toward gray they look natural, especially when combined with natural wood tones or other natural elements like tile, stonework, and plants. Since these blues are sometimes referred to as "spa" colors, their variations work well in bedrooms and bathrooms because of their calming effect.

▲ SMOKY BLUE WALLS in this light-filled entry complement the warm wood tones and emphasize the unique arched doorway. Reminiscent of the sea, the blue color makes a good backdrop for the model ship on the shelf.

◀ BATHROOMS CAN NATURALLY feel cold. To counteract the effects of the coolness, a warm golden-neutral color was used on the walls to complement the tiles.

◄ A TONED, COUNTRY BLUE contrasts with the white ceiling, emphasizing the dramatic vault and the windows in this room. The combination of painted woodwork used with natural wood tones works well because the finishes are limited.

▼ THE VARIETY OF BLUES, grays, and browns in the slate flooring were the starting point for the color scheme in this kitchen. The blue-gray island cabinets complement the floor but also add natural texture that mimics the wood ceiling.

Fresh and Clean

B LUES THAT ARE light and crisp—but not pale—are perfect when teamed up with white to reinforce the fresh look they bring to any room. In fact, white is better than beige or taupe because it appears more "clean." These blues also work well with other tints or tones of the same blue to add a bit more strength but maintain the fresh feeling. Because of their clean look, these blues work well in bathrooms and laundry rooms.

Many people think that these shades of blue are too cool to be used in large amounts. But when combined with the right accent colors, like light yellow and peach, these blues take on warm tones and provide the clean look they're known for.

▲ BECAUSE THERE'S SO MUCH visual wall space in this bedroom, including interesting windows and a French door, painting the ceiling the same blue as the walls would have been overwhelming. White ceiling and white trim freshen the scene.

Blue is a color that looks best when combined with white or lighter wood tones, which gives a room a fresh, crisp look that is difficult to achieve with dark woodwork.

▲ WHEN PALE COLORS are used, contrast is often needed to keep a room from appearing bland. The dark finish of the furniture against the cool blue walls gives this bedroom a contemporary and dramatic look. The blue color is repeated in the ceiling recess to draw attention to the architectural detail and tie the open space together.

◄ A REFRESHING BLUE HUE used for the sofa as well as the wall color is punctuated by the painted trim. The dark finish of the chair legs and drapery rods provides needed contrast.

Sophisticated

AS WITH THE OTHER shades of blue, sophisticated blues are also calming and relaxing but are in shades that are more dramatic than the pale blues while more subtle than the brights. These blues tend to work best with traditional furnishings, pearlized finishes, subtle metallics, and sumptuous fabrics, like iridescent silk, giving a traditional setting an elegant feeling.

Whether pale or deep, these blues require some light neutrals with them, usually a creamy color, not white, since the cream reinforces the sophistication of the blue tones. These blue shades also pair nicely with golden brown, which raises the temperature of the blue while complementing it, making any room feel cozy.

▲ GREAT ARCHITECTURE IS enhanced by contrasting colors that define the walls and woodwork. The regal blue wall color emphasizes the generous moldings and shows off the gold color of the mirror, wall sconces, and picture frame.

◄ MEDIUM TO PALE blue tones, ivory, and cream are combined for a sophisticated, restful combination in this bedroom. The addition of the light-colored fabric that forms the bed treatment helps to keep the room light and provides contrast against the blue walls.

◄ DEEP BLUE WALLS in this powder room make the framed mirror sparkle with elegance. The white wood trim and the light finish of the vanity cabinet and chair provide contrast, add light, and keep the room from looking too dark.

▼ INSPIRED BY ONE of the colors in the original stained-glass window, pale blue is the dominant color for the dining room in this turn-of-the-century Victorian house. The reflective properties of the crystal chandelier, glass tabletop, and silk drapery fabric gives this room a light, not heavy quality. The once-dark wood trim painted in a pearlized cream contributes to the effect.

COLOR SCHEMES THAT WORK

Blue is warmed up here by the use of a large amount of warm neutrals and camel colors. Depending on your locale, it's a good idea to bring in some warm colors to counteract the effects of such a cool color. If you live in a hot tropical climate, you can use more cool colors than if you live in a cooler climate, where too many of these colors may feel cold.

USING A PLAIN fabric for the larger furniture pieces gives a room stability and a place for your eyes to rest. Because this room uses several different patterns, a plain fabric is needed for the largest piece of furniture, in this case the sofa. However, the ribbed surface adds texture and variety.

A BLUE-AND-CAMEL striped fabric adds stability to this living room. Its strong geometric pattern works well with the busy pattern in the rug. The same stripe is used again for a pillow on the sofa, this time on the diagonal. Don't overlook the possibilities of using striped fabrics in different ways.

A MID-VALUE blue wall completes the picture. Wall color should be chosen last, after all the fabrics have been selected. It's much easier to have paint mixed to just the right color than it is to find fabrics to go with an existing wall color.

A SOFT PLAID is used for the draperies, combining several shades of the neutral colors. Dark wood drapery rods mirror the finish on the cocktail table for added contrast.

THE FLORAL PRINT fabric in the chairs combines the same colors but in softer, muted tones. The blue in the fabric is barely visible from a distance but is apparent up close. Because the floral pattern is not strong, it doesn't compete with the rug.

The Hotel Book

Dream pools & gardens

AMERICAN
IMPRESSIONISM

Purple

O f all the colors, purple is one of the most powerful and the most intriguing. It's a color that can steal the scene, no matter where it's used. Reactions to this color vary from meditative to magical, energizing to irritating. It can be uplifting and optimistic when used in the right strength, or if it's too dark and muddy, edging toward black, it can be dreary and depressing.

Technically termed "violet," purple is a secondary color that is midway between blue and red, at the end of the visible color spectrum. Purple falls into the "cool" category, but because it contains characteristics of both blue and red, it can help a room become more of one characteristic than the other based on how it's used and what colors it is paired with. Deep purple, such as eggplant, is rich and sophisticated while lighter versions of purple, such as lilac and lavender, have the similar restful qualities of blue but without the chill.

Full strength, purple is typically associated with contemporary furnishings, but when it's tinted, as in violet or lilac, or toned, as in plum or magenta, it becomes a color that works well with most other colors and in all types of decorating styles. If you're considering purple for your home, whether your style is contemporary or traditional, don't forget to use some contrasting values or colors. It's the playful interaction of light and dark, old and new, high and low that keeps a purple room looking fresh.

◄ RED-VIOLET, PURPLE, AND BLUE team well together, since they are next to one another on the color wheel. The rosy-purple in the accents, from the rug to the lamp and flowers, is repeated, but the deep purple is what grabs your attention.

Bold and Adventurous

PEOPLE WHO USE the brighter hues of purple tend to have a lot of creativity, a sense of adventure, and may be extroverts, with lively and vivacious personalities. You'll find that their home is probably full of color. Those who love purple also tend to love red and often will use the two together. Purples that are strong and bright or deep and toned also work well with hot pink, lime green, bright blue, orange, and yellow.

Strong shades of purple have been found to stimulate creativity and activity, making them appropriate in a family room, playroom, or even home office. Combined with yellow, they may even help you stay motivated while working and improve memory. Strong purples probably aren't the best choice in a nursery, child's bedroom, or a study, where relaxation is desired. Paler versions or smaller amounts of purple work better in those kinds of rooms. If you love the color but don't want to use a lot of purple, try it out in just a few accents. A purple glass bowl can add impact to a yellow or red dining room or kitchen, while purple pillows can punch up a green sofa.

DEEP ROYAL-PURPLE cabinets are daring enough but really pop with the addition of a bright orange-red on the inside and on the knobs. A medium-value green trim surrounds the clerestory windows, while a paler shade of green trims the windows beyond. The lighter green works to keep the windows from appearing "boxy" while it accents the yellow walls and keeps the space feeling light.

PAINTING THE WALLS purple in the bathroom is one way to get attention. But with the end wall neutral, the vibrant purple doesn't overwhelm the space or close it in, keeping the eye moving around the room.

◀ AN UNEXPECTED CHOICE for a hallway, the deep purple walls make a strong backdrop for the varying shades of blue furniture. The area rug contributes pattern and helps to unify the color scheme. Visual relief comes from the white trim; if it had been stained dark, the space would have a heavier, dark feeling.

Purples

Purple encourages creativity, and because of this, artists and musicians are drawn to the color. It's also associated with high ideals, as well as loyalty, religion, ritual, and spirituality. Purple is also an emotional color that can stir our basic feelings. When used in paler versions, it's an ethereal color. When used full-strength, it works best with a little green, brown, or gold added to help keep things grounded.

◀ COLOR IS NOT CONSTANT. The light from the windows on the stairway lightens that portion of the colored wall. Contributing to that is the reflective quality of the white wall. The color beneath the stairway appears darker due to the fact that it is shadowed by the stairs.

▼ WHILE ALMOST ANY COLOR could work here, the soft lavender hue is pretty and restful, and makes for a good place to work on all kinds of projects without distracting or being hard on the eyes.

Did You Know...

A room's function should help inform the colors you select. You don't want too harsh a color, since that can cause eye strain. Pick the color you like at a fairly intense level, and then tone it down a bit to a slightly "dirtier" hue.

◀ NOT YOUR TYPICAL kitchen colors, purple and turquoise make for a striking combination here. The upper cabinets showcase accessories that were carefully selected to emphasize the colors and enhance the palette.

▼ A VIVID PURPLE SOFA would look out of place if it were the only purple item in the room. Because the drapery and ottoman fabrics contain purple, the scheme is unified. The warm neutrals of the wall, ceiling, and carpet help to soften the look.

◀ CONTEMPORARY COLOR MEETS traditional detailing in this home office. The purple cabinet fronts add just enough liveliness to the stained woodwork, giving this space an unexpected combination of finishes. If the cabinets and drawers were all stained brown, the result would have been more ordinary.

BLACK FURNITURE AND a light floor help to balance the purple, teal-blue, and coral-pink colors. The carpet color lightens the palette, while the black furniture makes the other colors seem more intense and dramatic.

FOUR MAIN COLORS were chosen for this kid's room—purple, blue, orange, and lime green. Lighter tints of the same colors on the walls provide consistency. The Roman shades, made out of two different colors, creatively solves a problem window and emphasizes the line of the ceiling, which was kept white to keep the room from feeling closed in.

THE ASSORTED COLORS of the buoys suspended from the ceiling were inspiration for this kid's room. The repetition of the shapes creates a feeling of rhythm and motion in this space where a multitude of colors are used. Knotty pine flooring and paneling on the ceiling contribute to the causal feeling.

PERIWINKLE, a combination of purple and blue, is applied to the walls in wide stripes that alternate with white and is used again on the floor to carry out this color scheme. The whimsical pattern on the bedding brings in the complementary colors for a bright and youthful look.

Did You Know...

Wood floors can be the perfect place to have fun with color. Floors can be painted a solid color or contain stripes, squares, diamonds, or any other pattern; they can even be painted to simulate inlaid wood designs or intricate patterned "rugs."

COLOR SCHEMES THAT WORK

Bold use of color in this library is a reminder that color should be personal and fun. A scheme like this might be out of the question for the chromophobic, but it will make others jump for joy. All the colors—from the orange, yellow, and purple fabrics to those on the spines of the books—play a role in the color scheme. The natural light from the expansive window floods the room and serves to balance the heaviness of the bookcase.

A DEEP PURPLE chenille throw, the same color as the bookcases, makes the orange of the sofa less powerful.

THE CARPET, similar in hue to the sofas, provides texture and adds more coziness. A tile or wood floor would have made this space feel cold.

SOFAS COVERED in an orange, finely textured chenille fabric give the room a warm, inviting look.

A TEXTURED purple ottoman used opposite the purple bookcases uses its color to balance the room.

PURPLE, PEACH, AND YELLOW pillows provide subtle contrast. The yellow adds a touch of brightness and plays off the complementary color, purple.

Sophisticated

PURPLES THAT FALL in the sophisticated range are complex, meaning they are made up of a combination of varying hues of other colors, but are duller. While this means they're less powerful than the bright purples they're attention-grabbing nonetheless. When teamed up with taupe, neutrals, black, and most shades of green, these purples can border on gray or take on an eggplant hue. Mixed with red, they can move toward deep berry colors that are sometimes hard to differentiate between burgundy and purple. These shades of purple work well in living rooms and bedrooms, and provide a great background for showing off artwork since they let other elements in a room take center stage. Used as accents, wall color, or even on cabinetry, these purples don't shout at you but have a definite presence.

▶ THIS MONOCHROMATIC ROOM features tints and shades of purple from deep purple to pale lavender. If all the furniture were in the same tone, the result would have been boring, but because of the variety of values, the room is interesting and sophisticated.

▼ DEEP, RICH PLUM TONES are combined with warm neutrals to give this room a sophisticated and subtle look. A minimal amount of the rich plum color, which is between purple and red, was used to keep the feeling regal but not overly dramatic.

Did You Know...

Dark colors have more visual weight than light colors. Pay attention to where you use dark colors in your home to make sure the colors look balanced. If you have a large item in a dark color or finish, for example a deep purple sofa, place something with equal "weight" on the other side of the room—a wood cabinet, desk, large painting, or another upholstered item, such as a chair.

◄ COMBINED WITH natural wood tones, purple base cabinets anchor this large kitchen and add visual weight. If the reverse had been done, with the purple on the upper cabinets, the room would have looked top heavy. Red knobs on the stove act as punctuation marks and give the room personality.

Understated

PURPLE IS BEAUTIFUL used in dark or light hues, but will result in completely different moods. Pale and toned-down purples that sometimes look pink, lilac, or orchid combine well with tints and shades of peach, pink, and greens, and will provide a softening effect. Similar to blues, they work well in rooms where you want quiet, like bedrooms or nurseries. But be warned: Some believe that very light tints of purple, such as lilac or orchid, can drain your energy. Others believe that too much of very light purple in a room will disconnect you from the world around you because it's too ethereal. Pairing brown with those lighter shades of purple works well to ground the color scheme and keep it from being too otherworldly. If you opt to use a monochromatic scheme in any purple hue, but particularly with the understated versions, be sure to include some neutrals, since they help to add freshness or contrast to the scheme.

▲ THIS PALE LILAC and white combination is an easy-to-do color scheme. Always a good choice for a bedroom, the use of one soft color plus white can make a room feel restful. In addition, distracting pattern is kept to a minimum. The warm color of the wood floor works to keep the room from looking sterile and adds warmth.

◄ LOG-STYLE HOMES typically feel masculine, but thanks to the bedcovering and soft purple blinds, this one has a subtle touch of femininity. The large-scale plaid that introduces pink and purple respects the character and style of the home.

▲ SOFT VIOLETS, LILAC, purples, and pinks contribute to this pleasant, restful bedroom. Since the colors are all from a similar family with only the strength of each varied, the combination is guaranteed to work.

Red

N o other color commands attention like red. Red turns heads. The fashion
industry has always understood the power of the red dress, and the sexy
appeal of red lips, fingernails, and red high heels. It is associated with excitement, power, danger, love, and romance. The hottest of all colors, it is by far the most
interesting, stimulating, and mysterious.

In the home, red can send powerful messages as well. Have you ever been in a room
with all red walls? How did you feel? Did it make you feel energized, anxious, irritated,
or hungry? Depending on which shade of red and the amount used in that room, you
could have experienced any of those emotions.

Whether your decorating style incorporates antiques or chrome and glass, any
furniture style can take advantage of the power of red. Take, for example, an antique
Chinese-red lacquered chest with old-world charm. Used in a traditional setting with
floral prints and 18th-century pieces, the red is appropriate. Take that same red hue
and paint it on the walls in a glossy finish in an urban loft, and the look is just the opposite, yet works just as well.

◀ USING ONE COLOR throughout a space is a good way to unify an eclectic room. Even
though this house is traditional, the color brings together Asian and modern elements.

◀ BECAUSE YELLOW IS a highly reflective color and red tends to read as "dark" the two colors are powerful when combined. In this room each color is used in almost equal amounts, giving the space a visually balanced look.

▶ USING RED ON YOUR WALLS can work to show off an art collection and add drama. With neutral upholstery and carpet, the red accent pillows and red welting on the ottoman hold the scheme together and make the art stand out.

▼ A CONTROLLED AMOUNT OF RED added to any room can contribute a happy, lively feeling. The window treatment in this attic bedroom takes away any dreary feeling that an attic might otherwise have.

MOODMAKERS

Reds

Red has been proven to increase blood pressure and speed up the heart rate and respiration. It's also been shown to increase the appetite and can actually make you hungry. It may be too stimulating for a bedroom in highly saturated hues, but can feel rich and elegant when muted.

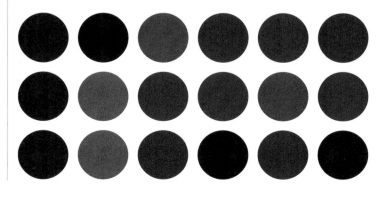

Bold and Daring

BOLD REDS CAN REALLY HEAT UP a room. They become daring when they're used in large amounts, such as on the walls, or as a dramatic splash of color that becomes the focal point. These strong, highly saturated reds can be blue-based for a cool look or orange-based for a warm effect.

If the idea of using one of these strong reds for an entire room appeals to you, just be aware of how that might make you feel. Sometimes these intense reds are often best in smaller rooms where you don't spend a lot of time, like a powder room, because they can make you feel nervous. In addition, when combined with highly contrasting trim, they seem brighter and stronger than when used with stained finishes or trim that's painted a deeper tone. Whether combined with black accents or neutrals, the color is bound to draw attention.

◄ THIS VIBRANT RED KITCHEN is stimulating and inviting. Softened by fabrics on the windows, the cabinets stand out but seem mellow against the wood plank flooring. This red value is perfect for traditional country-style elements.

▲ BECAUSE THE WALL COLOR and the natural woodwork are close in value, the red takes on a more subtle tone than if the woodwork had been painted either a light or dark color.

▲ DESPITE ITS STRENGTH, the red walls don't overpower this room. Since it's used behind the bookcase, it makes the light trim stand out. Additionally, the ceiling detail calls attention away from the walls and adds interest.

▲ PAINTING JUST ONE WALL in a bright color is a great way to introduce personality without going overboard. If the bright red had been used on all four walls of this bedroom, the space would have been too stimulating.

▷ SMALL TOUCHES OF RED, inspired by the stove, are used on the windows and bring this kitchen to life. Because the valences are mounted all the way up to the ceiling, they make the ceiling appear higher.

▲ DEEP RED WALLS surround this reading nook and make it warm and cozy, especially when the light casts a warm, intimate glow. The neutral fabric and black picture frame make this a fairly relaxing area, even though the red is a stimulating color.

◀ A CRIMSON STAIRWAY in this contemporary house is art on its own. Intended to stand out against neutral walls, the zigzag pattern formed by the stairs is emphasized by the red color.

Classic

N EITHER HOT NOR COLD, classic reds are slightly toned down and almost "neutral," as far as red goes. Regardless of how they're used, they won't dominate the way brighter reds will. Reds that fall into this category are so appealing that they work well in dining rooms or livings rooms—places where you'll spend a lot of time. And they combine particularly well with blues, yellows, and greens to create a traditional setting.

If you want to try out just a bit of red, look for a fabric you love with a pattern that contains some red. Then pull the red out through your accessories. While you want to make sure the reds you use throughout the room are similar in their hue, value, and intensity, think also about the contrast. A red-patterned fabric on a white or yellow background is going to appear much stronger (and also busier) than if it were on a background of mid to deep tones. Likewise, using a solid red for an upholstered piece will seem more intense against a light background. If you want to use red in a subtle manner, avoid extreme contrast and limit its use to small objects.

▲ COLOR CAN COME FROM the furniture itself and here it takes center stage. The classic Chinese form and red color of the buffet make this piece a focal point, but because the wood tones in the room are equally as strong, it doesn't seem out of place.

▼ BURGUNDY-RED CHAIRS and lamp give this library consistent color yet don't demand too much attention. Their masculine feel enlivens the space while providing a warm, inviting look.

▲ THE RED-STAINED PANELING is reminiscent of a barn, enveloping this country-style dining area. In contrast, the wood trim around the doors and windows are painted white to emphasize the windows and to highlight the red color.

Sophisticated

THESE HIGH-STYLE VERSIONS of red, which include toned-down burgundy as well as bright berry, can look soft and understated when combined with mid-value neutrals or more dramatic when used with white. These reds have a complex and intriguing effect that can work well in almost any type of room because they are not as highly stimulating as the more intense reds.

These reds don't scream for attention but get it anyway. They tend to feel more earthy than other reds and have an almost natural appeal that works well with earthy greens, browns, and neutrals. For the conservative taste, use them to add character to traditional furnishings. For a more daring look, use them to show off important art and also give an intimate feeling to a room.

▲ DEEP BRICK RED WALLS give this living room an intimate, inviting look. Because the art, console table, and walls have a similar tonal value, the look is understated, not jarring.

◄ OFTEN FORGOTTEN, the ceiling is a place where creativity can be expressed. A painted compass using a dominant red color draws attention to this library ceiling and adds character.

Did You Know...

Complementary colors will intensify each other when used close together. Known as one of Chevreul's Laws, each color tints its neighbor with its own complement, making both appear more intense than if viewed alone. A strong red will appear even more intense if placed next to an equally strong green. Sometimes colors will appear to vibrate, causing unpleasant sensations.

Did You Know...

Warm, tonal reds can create a sense of intimacy and warmth, while highly saturated reds used in large amounts can make you nervous.

▲ A TRADITIONAL ASIAN wallpaper provides color and style in this mainly white bathroom. Small amounts of blue in both the wall tiles and wallpaper give the room a cohesive look.

COLOR SCHEMES THAT WORK

Reds and browns make up this handsome color scheme, unified by the floral print. Because the colors are dark, light carpeting and woodwork keep the room from feeling oppressive. The crown molding, stained a deep tone, makes a good transition between the walls and the ceiling.

AN OPTIONAL wall color for this room could have been brown, but may have made the room look dreary. By using red on the walls, the room has vibrancy and warmth.

DARK RED leather was chosen for the ottoman/ cocktail table, giving the room a classic look. If a brighter red had been used, it would have stood out, but here, the color is in the same general family as the wall color, only toned down.

A BROWN-TEXTURED fabric, chosen for the sofa, repeats the background color of the floral print. Since the floral print is used so many times in the room, the plain fabric keeps the room from looking too busy.

THIS FLORAL PRINT, containing brown, red, and green, was chosen first, with the color scheme of the room built around it. It's obvious that red and brown are the dominant colors in the room. Since multicolored fabrics often present many more options than ones with one or two colors, the same fabric could have been used with brown walls and green fabric on the furniture.

RED PAINT is one of the most difficult colors to apply on walls. Make sure you start with a tinted primer, and don't be alarmed if the look of the first coat isn't what you expected. Red paint often requires several coats for good coverage. Allow several days or more for the paint to dry completely.

THE WARM, light wood tone of the trim is actually a color that's part of the floral print, giving the room a cohesive look and keeping things light.

Fun and Bright

REDS THAT BORDER ON pink or orange give a room a sense of adventure and reveal a willingness to play with color. They pair well with yellow and purple. While these reds are playful and youthful, they need some neutrals added to separate the colors or they can feel overwhelming. Fun and bright reds work well in kitchens and family rooms, where there's activity and creativity.

Having said that, these reds can be a bit intense, so are often best used in small amounts, such as pillows, valances, or vases. But don't automatically discount the idea of using them in large amounts. If you want to use one of these reds in a big way, just make sure that the rest of your house has a few touches of equal vibrancy—a room full of bright color needs to be able to transition into other rooms. The best way of accomplishing this is by using some of the same, bright colors in the adjoining room, even if it's only in small amounts.

▲ A LITTLE RED goes a long way to brighten up this kitchen. The detail on the backs of the red metal bar stools is emphasized against the painted cabinetry and neutral backgrounds; the wood floor adds to the casual feeling.

◄ RED, WHITE, AND BLUE are combined to make this kid's room lively. Colored furniture is a good way to add splashes of color throughout a room; white cabinetry keeps things light, while the deep blue carpet adds practicality by hiding dirt.

▲ A HOME OFFICE should be comfortable yet motivating. Deep royal blue and red provide the right amount of both stimulation and relaxation since they're provided in accents in the seating area, not around the actual work space.

▶ MULTIPLE COLORS USED in unusual ways gives this traditional wood kitchen an up-to-date feel. Red accents throughout the room keep the eye moving around the open space.

▼ BRIGHT BLOCKS OF COLOR against pure white walls and a dark, polished floor give this room a strong and confident look. Even the painting repeats the theme of the wall cabinet and makes the red chairs pop.

◄ IF AN ALL-WHITE bathroom or kitchen is just too colorless for your taste, use small accents of color in the room. The tile came first in this bath, but the colorful knobs and pulls, wall hooks, and ottoman all contribute to tie the scheme together.

► PRIMARY COLORS ARE a good choice for kids' spaces, as evidenced by this Adirondack-style bunkhouse. When used in the right amount and décor, red can easily take on a rustic feeling.

COLOR SCHEMES THAT WORK

Bright colors abound in this entry but none seem to overpower the space. This is because they're all used at the same intensity. The valence ties the other colors together and the white trim punctuates the space with freshness.

BECAUSE THE HIGHLY saturated colors are printed on a white fabric background, they appear brighter than if they were on a toned, dull one.

RED IS THE DOMINANT color in this entry, so red pillows work well to continue the theme. Yellow, the opposite of purple, works well as an accent, here in pillows, because it's the complement to purple, and it adds light.

DEEP COLORS are great for rugs because they hide dirt; this bright purple geometric rug also adds a colorful accent.

THE WHITE TRIM color contributes a fresh quality to the room and highlights the wall color. The baseboard heater is painted the same as the trim color, making it almost a part of the woodwork and ensuring that it doesn't stand out. The white beadboard ceiling brings in texture.

THE VIBRANT red wall emits energy and warmth. If you are hesitant about using such a strong color in a primary room, try using it in a less dominant part of the house like a hallway or bathroom.

PURPLE is repeated in the pillow on the bench.

Pink

Although pink is actually a tint of red, it's popular and versatile in its own right and is being fully embraced in the home. While it can be too feminine for some tastes, it has a lot of personality and pairs well with many other colors. Pink can work alone or with other colors to create a room that is soft and sweet, sophisticated, or strong and vibrant.

Created by mixing red with white, very pale pinks can elicit a feeling of being drained; in fact, powdery pinks are perfect for the bedroom, since they can help to induce sleep; warmer pinks, like rose pink, make the mood for a room more positive and uplifting, and can even be motivating. Bright, hot pink can be too stimulating when used in large amounts, so beware of this when choosing the color as part of your decorating scheme.

Because pink has good reflective qualities, it gives skin a healthy appearance, making this color a good choice for bathrooms. It works best when used with incandescent, not fluorescent, lighting, though. Pink used in a bathroom should be on the warm side, not a more cold blue-pink.

PINK AND YELLOW are used in almost equal proportions in this young girl's room, giving it a sunny and calming feeling. Any more pink would be too much and could look overly "sugary." The white woodwork keeps the room fresh and provides a resting place for the eye.

Soft and Sweet

PINKS THAT FALL IN THE SOFT AND SWEET, or calming range, are pastels that are clear and clean. Because these pinks bring the word "pretty" to mind, they are often used in bedrooms, particularly a girl's room. Pale pink walls combined with white lace bedding and small pink and green prints give a bedroom a romantic, nostalgic look.

Using these pale pinks in other rooms in the house can be tricky because of their decidedly feminine appeal. Whether used in a family room or bedroom, the pale nature of these pinks can be downplayed when they're combined with green, blue, or purple in large amounts. As with all colors, the furniture, accents, and lighting complete a look, but your lifestyle and how you use a room is also an important influence. While it's unlikely that pink will ever be masculine in feeling, it can take on different moods based on the makeup of the space as well as the style of the furnishings.

▲ PUTTY-COLORED PANELING instead of white gives this room a country feeling and grounds the pink. Because there's less of a contrast between the wall color and the pink chaise, the pink doesn't seem so strong or so feminine. White paneling would have made the pink more dominant.

◄ WHILE THE MULTICOLORED chair features four colors that are also repeated around the room, the pink becomes a bit more dominant thanks to the large bed skirt and touches of pink in multiple shades.

Did You Know...

You can use several different patterns together in a room as long as the colors are compatible and the scale of the patterns is not all the same.

▲ THIS MONOCHROMATIC BEDROOM uses tints and tones of the red and pink families to give the room variety. The many different patterns, from plaids to florals, stripes to solids, work well together because of their unified color and varying scale.

► THE DARK WOOD TONES of the sofa, floor, and clock help to keep this room from feeling too feminine. In fact, the high contrast between the wood and pink makes this room feel balanced.

MOODMAKERS

Pinks

Soft, pale pinks are often associated with babies or little girls. Rosier pinks, often used in the Victorian era, are romantic and lady-like. But take pink over to the brighter side, and it becomes energizing and active, much like the stronger reds. Soft and calming, or intense and stimulating, there's a version of pink for everyone.

COLOR SCHEMES THAT WORK

Flattering blush tones and white give this bedroom a quiet and calming feeling. With all the woodwork painted white, the woven, natural sisal floor covering adds needed texture that keeps the room from looking flat.

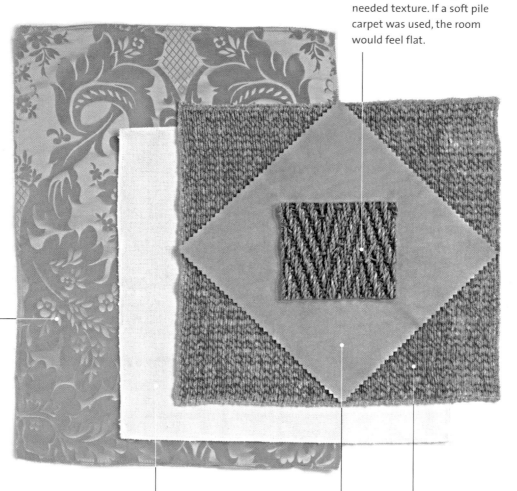

SISAL FLOOR covering adds needed texture. If a soft pile carpet was used, the room would feel flat.

THE ROSY PINK hue of the quilt and trim on the comforter provides the most color impact in this bedroom. Because the quilt is patterned, the color is more subtle than if the quilt were a solid.

WHITE LINEN on the bedskirt and headboard add a crisp, fresh look and provides subtle texture.

SOFT PINK pillows add just enough color to keep the room from looking too colorless.

Sophisticated

SOPHISTICATED PINKS are decidedly different from the pale and sweet pinks because they are slightly "dirtier" than the soft pinks, meaning not as clean and crisp. Ranging from rose to peachy-pink and flesh tones, these pinks have a more mature look that works well in a variety of rooms. A monochromatic combination of several different tints and tones of midtone pinks to pale pinks can give a room a subtle and sophisticated look. When this kind of scheme is used, gray or taupe will help to keep the room from becoming too overwhelmingly pink. To create a completely different look, combine deep colors like brown or navy blue with these pinks, which act almost like a neutral; these schemes are suitable for living rooms and dining rooms. Whichever route you go, play around with different combinations and intensities of colors until you find the one that suits you best and achieves the effect you're looking for.

▲ A COMBINATION OF neutral color with bits of a subtle color as accents helps to keep a room clean and cozy, as evidenced in this bedroom. The rose color is used enough throughout the room to make its choice deliberate.

◀ THE FLORAL, TEA-STAINED FABRIC adds a nostalgic look to this dining room. The mid-value rose color found in the fabric was also used on the walls and woodwork to unify the room. The circular arrangement of plates brings contemporary flair to this otherwise traditional room.

◀ THE COLORFUL RUG is the inspiration for the color scheme in this room. The black background in the rug makes the other colors pop, and since the brightest colors are on the floor, it keeps the eye grounded in the space.

▼ THE CHARMING, CURVED window and architectural detailing demands the primary attention in this living room. The pillows add just enough color to draw the eye toward the space and soften the lines of the window without detracting from its elegance.

◀ A POWDER ROOM is the perfect place to use bold or deep color because not a lot of time is spent in this room. This deep pink powder room is elegant, thanks to the style of the fixtures and window treatments, as well as the simplicity of the space.

COLOR SCHEMES THAT WORK

This highly sophisticated color scheme is a good example of using two main colors together successfully. The vibrant pink and medium brown are used individually throughout the room but are then brought together in the sofa fabric to tie the color scheme together.

RASPBERRY SILK side panels frame the windows and contrast against the brown walls and white trim. The silk adds a bit of roughness, complementing the velvety sofa fabric.

MILK CHOCOLATE walls add depth and drama, and ensure this living space doesn't feel too feminine.

A SOFTLY patterned rug in brown, pink, and other neutral colors reinforces the color scheme yet lets the other uses of color command the attention.

RASPBERRY-COLORED velvet used for one of the sofas is repeated on the windows, adding the right amount of visual punch.

THE DAMASK pattern is not only appropriate for the style of the sofa but features the room's two main colors in bold tones.

THIS FLORAL PRINT contains all the ingredients for a successful color scheme since it combines both main colors used in the room. Although not much of the print is used, it's enough to tie together the color scheme.

Strong and Vibrant

I F YOU LOVE BRIGHT PINKS, use them in any room. These strong and vivid colors have similar effects to red—they are energizing and stimulating and work well with other bright colors. Bright pinks don't have the feminine and babyish qualities or pale pinks, especially when they're combined with other strong, bright colors and neutrals.

Hot pink, like fuchsia, used as an accent color can add life and energy to any room, but too much of it can be irritating. It's a good color in controlled amounts, for almost any room. Try your favorite bright pink with light to bright greens and purple. Or use it with other warm colors like red, yellow, and orange for a really hot look. Used just for accents with neutrals, these bright pinks can add life to a plain room. Keep in mind that bright pinks work best with contemporary styling.

▲ CORAL CAN BE WARM when combined with the right colors, such as the green, taupe, and white used in this bedroom. This shade of pink is intense but not too sweet, making it a good choice for an adult space.

◀ DEEP, DARK CHOCOLATE BROWN lacquered walls add drama and intimacy, while shocking pink pillows keep the room from being dull and dark. Texture also plays a large role here, from the smooth, reflective sheen of the walls to the sisal rug, sofa fabric, and plant.

Did You Know...

Flowers can reinforce a room's color scheme. Take note: The colors don't have to match, and when they are in a complementary color, they can make a dull color scheme more lively. For example, in a room that's mainly blue, a floral arrangement that contains some oranges and yellows can enliven the space.

▲ NOT YOUR TYPICAL DINING ROOM color, the pleasant rosy pink walls give this room a soft, calming feeling. With the same tone of color repeated on the chairs, this room is easy on the eyes. The darker wood floor provides needed contrast and helps to anchor the room.

▲ THE SOFT, TYPICALLY FEMININE color scheme in this kitchen creates a different personality when combined with heavy, rustic beams and wood flooring. The high ceilings and natural light help to keep the space feeling airy, so that just the right amount of attention is given to the pastel colors.

▲ IN A CONTEMPORARY SPACE like this, a little pattern and lots of color are all that's needed to make a statement. The deep blue wall in the background is equally as strong as the pink of the chairs. In contrast, the remaining walls are kept neutral.

▲ A CHECKERBOARD OF carpet squares puts the attention on the floor of this bedroom for a bold and modern look. Instead of using the bright pink color on the walls, a pale version was chosen to soften the look.

▶ WHEN CHOOSING PAINT COLOR for a room with a lot of woodwork, it's important to pay close attention to the color of the wood. It's often best to choose a color that's opposite the wood color rather than close to it to bring out the color of the wood rather than compete with it.

▲ A COMBINATION OF hot pink and orange give this living room a daring look. The neutral off-white color of the chair, woodwork, and walls gives the eye a place to rest, but also makes the colors stand out.

◄ TYPICALLY IN A LOG HOME like this you'd expect to see natural or subdued colors. The hot pink and off-white colors are a delightful surprise.

▲ USE RESTRAINT with a powerful color. Since the hot pink and white harlequin pattern was used on only one wall the result is lively and fun. If the pattern had been continued on the walls around the room, the effect would be dizzying.

◄ A GUEST ROOM IS the perfect place to be bold. Pink and green is a natural combination, and coupled with the dark headboards doesn't seem overly feminine here.

COLOR SCHEMES THAT WORK

This room successfully combines neutrals for the main upholstered pieces with colorful accents to enliven the space. The pale pink walls, while not what you might call a true neutral, warm up the room with just a hint of color and keep the mood calm and reflective. White trim adds freshness.

A NEUTRAL, taupe-colored texture is used for the sofa, allowing for the introduction of colorful accent pillows.

AS ANOTHER accent, a green fabric with a tonal pattern is used to bring out the green in the rug.

PALE PINK faux suede is used to cover the square ottoman, linking it to the wall color. If the walls had not been painted this same color, the ottoman would look like it didn't belong.

A ROSY CORAL fabric, a stronger version of the wall color, is used here for a pillow, adding brightness to the room.

A BRIGHT BLUE chenille throw is added on top of the taupe chair, creating a lively look and bringing in a burst of color that mimics the blue in the rug.

THE CHAIR is covered in a slightly deeper taupe than the sofa. The texture of the smooth, shiny silk and the dull, nubby chenille on the sofa create seemingly conflicting textures that work to enhance the look of the room.

THIS FRENCH-STYLE "Savonnerie" rug sets the tone for the room and plays off the French fireplace. The muted colors of taupe, green, pink, and blue add subtle pattern and design to the room.

Orange

Y ou've probably never seen an all-orange room. In fact, because it's most associated with energy and excitement, orange is often used for sports equipment. But orange is also considered a friendly color that stimulates conversation. This hot color has also been found to stimulate the appetite, so restaurants like to use toned-down versions. In the home, there are many opportunities to bring in this lively color.

The most common shades of orange in the home are peach, salmon, terra-cotta, shrimp, rust, cinnamon, and brown, but brighter shades of orange are making their way into the home as well. Like red and pink, certain shades are flattering to skin tones and work well in bathrooms and bedrooms. But in its brightest form orange also can make a room feel too hot. With this in mind, homes in warm climates need to be balanced with cool colors, such as turquoise, greens, and all shades of blues.

Thirty years ago orange was popular and was typically used in bold floral prints and combined with brown or yellow. The oranges found in homes and home furnishings today are either really bright and clear or pale and toned. For a modern look, try an intense orange with bright pink and lime green; for a softer, more livable look, use tonal oranges with neutrals, browns, or blues and greens.

◄ FIRST IMPRESSIONS COUNT. From the moment you enter a home, the color can set the mood for the entire house. The color in this entryway tells us there's lots of energy in this home. Since the woodwork and the floor are so dark, the bright orange brings life to the space.

Oranges

Orange, in its purest, brightest form, is an attention getter. Some people think of bright orange as looking "cheap," but in small amounts it can add flair. The toned-down versions, like terra cotta, can be calming and soothing, while earthy versions in copper are sophisticated.

▲ MOTHER NATURE PROVIDES great inspiration for a color scheme, as evidenced here in the natural stone. The gray trim highlights the subdued gray in the tile and contrasts nicely with the more primary copper-orange.

▶ CONTEMPORARY COLOR MEETS traditional furnishings in this living room. The painted traditionally styled fireplace mantel calls out for attention as the focal point while also adding contrast to the furniture and orangey-pink color scheme.

USING THIS MUCH ORANGE on your upholstery takes confidence, since it's not as easy to change as repainting a wall. The bright green rug and bold textural accents complete the energetic look.

Bold and Bright

BRIGHT ORANGES like tangerine, neon-orange, and carrot can have dramatic effects when used with contrasting colors like turquoise, black, and hot pink. Normally chosen for contemporary schemes, orange is a good choice when you want to add creative flair and punch to an ordinary room. How do you do this? Consider painting just one wall a lively shade of tangerine and then use a large dramatic painting to call further attention to the wall. Does that sound too bold? Cover a nightstand with a solid orange or orange-patterned table skirt, which can easily be removed or covered slightly to soften the look. Or use an orange fabric on your sofa or chairs.

Regardless of how much orange you bring into your home, be sure to counteract its stimulating effects by introducing a healthy dose of white or another neutral. This will bring necessary relief from the high energy level.

▲ ORANGE AND PURPLE, **an unexpected combination, decorate this traditional dining room and delight the eye. The two colors are visually blended together in the finely striped wallpaper.**

▲ A CREATIVE COMBINATION
of orange and green teams up on this stairway. A deeper, toned value of each color runs through the center of the stairs, resulting in a shadowy effect. A third, deeper green is used on the walls and is emphasized by the white trim on the stringers.

▶ IF YOU WANT TO **take a risk with a color scheme, go all the way! These three different colored chairs are only unified by their frame. The orange drapes and wall color add to the fun, lively theme.**

▲ BECAUSE THERE'S PLENTY of white to break things up, the hot orange and pink don't overwhelm. Orange, yellow, red, and pink are colors found near one another on the color wheel, making them work well together regardless of how bright their hue.

Toned and Sophisticated

TO BETTER UNDERSTAND what a toned-down orange is, close your eyes, picture orange, then make it earthy. Think dried leaves and clay, orange-based browns, and terra-cotta hues of autumn. These variations of orange—the timeless shades—are the most widely accepted, and they work well in most homes and in any type of room. Blues, greens, and turquoise of all tints and shades work well with these toned oranges and help add coolness to a scheme. Because they almost seem neutral, these oranges are not as trendy or as stimulating as the bright hues.

▼ A WARM, TERRA-COTTA–colored fabric on the sofa makes this cozy library inviting and intimate. If the sofa were a bright orange, the room would not feel as restful. The terra-cotta also appears in the area rug, helping to define the space.

▲ PEACHY-CINNAMON–COLORED WALLS, bordering on brown, warm up this large foyer; the color is carried through to the furnishings, from the hall table to the window seat cushion with pillows to the area rug. The different hues and tones add variety but not drama.

▲ AN EARTHY SALMON COLOR calls attention to the wall's sinuous, curving shape. The white recessed bookcases add emphasis, while the blue headboard provides straight-lined geometry to the room, complementing the curve of the wall and adding a cool touch.

► A RARE, COLORFUL MARBLE was the likely inspiration for the wall color in this bathroom. Earthy shades of orange were repeated throughout the room in the wall color, artwork, and accessories. Even the copper color of the sink and the wood tone contain hints of the orange color, making this a successful combination.

COLOR SCHEMES THAT WORK

Keeping your floor color and furnishings neutral allows you to try different walls colors—and change them if you don't like the look. This dining space works particularly well because the large window brings the foliage inside and adds both natural texture and green, which is a nice combination with the midtone orange.

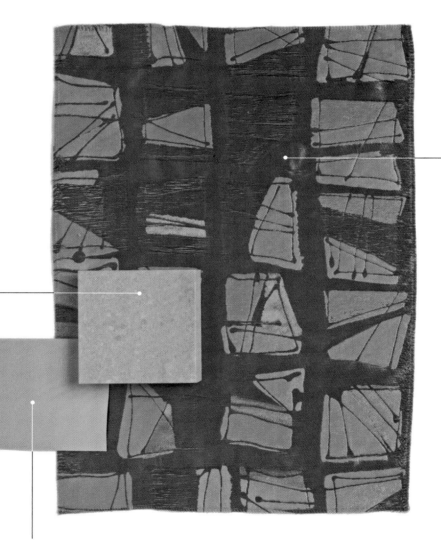

THIS NEUTRAL stone floor allows almost unlimited color choices. And, by carrying the same flooring from room to room, it gives the home a continuous "flow" that seems to enlarge spaces.

THE NEUTRAL fabric dining chairs add needed pattern and texture to the room. Since the orange walls and ceiling are so strong, keeping the chairs neutral brings necessary relief.

ORANGE-YELLOW, squash-colored walls give this room a golden glow. Continued on the ceiling, the color envelops the room and helps to bring the high ceiling down, giving the space a more intimate feeling.

Fun and Funky

MORE OF AN ATTITUDE than a color, fun and funky oranges are paired in unique combinations that have the energy and exuberance of youth. Often it's the *other* color that gives a room its character. Used with lime green, purple, or pink, orange can have the energy of a circus or give a room an offbeat appearance. These oranges can be bright or slightly off-orange, bordering on yellow and gold or moving toward red. These oranges can even seem fluorescent.

If you're having trouble committing to orange, try painting a flea market find in your favorite shade to see how much orange you can take. Then look at the other colors that you need to work with in the room to see if they look right with your new orange piece. Don't forget to consider your wood tones when looking at the colors of the room. If you like what you've done, go for it—and add a few other accents in the same color to keep your eye moving around the room.

▲ THIS CLOSET COLOR mirrors the clothes the home owner likes—bright and fun. This idea can be applied to other rooms—use a textural mid-tone orange for background, and add in white and other strong colors in a similar tone to keep the space consistent.

◄ DON'T BE AFRAID to try patterns that aren't true to the period of furniture. These traditional Victorian pieces are updated by brightly colored, graphic upholstery fabrics, resulting in a lively, young look for old furniture.

▲ THE COMBINATION OF orange and green is very natural—think a piece of fruit with leaves on it—and holds this kitchen together since they are repeated on the cabinets and trim. The orange ceiling gives the room a warm glow.

Classic and Conservative

PEACH AND SALMON, the softer, lighter versions of orange, are colors that most people find appealing. Because these oranges are not highly saturated, they don't contain the same energizing effects that the brighter versions do, and so their effect is similar to some shades of pink. All ranges of blues and greens work well with classic orange tones, and many traditional floral patterns will contain some amount of these colors. For an up-to-date look, use these colors as solids and textures on your major upholstery items.

▲ A MUTED ORANGE WALL creates the backdrop for a large, contemporary painting. The wall color is a slightly softer version of the chairs, which blend well with the wood tones used throughout the room.

◄ JUST A LITTLE TOUCH of color can take any neutral space from boring to dynamic. The back wall in this kitchen recess does just that, adding a splash of color to an otherwise stark space. If orange isn't your color, or if you just want to change your color scheme from time to time, try painting your backsplash in a lively color.

Did You Know...

Niches, recesses, soffits, and even the inside backs of cabinets and bookcases are all good places to try out colors. In small amounts, brighter and deeper colors can make a room come alive and may be just the thing the room needs.

▼ PEACH, CINNAMON, AND BROWN are versions of orange that work well together since they are natural and earthy colors. The orange wall here adds a burst of energy.

Yellow

ellow, the color that seems to be infused with light, makes most people feel happy. A room that's filled with yellow fills us with warmth because it reminds us of sunlight. Pale and buttery or bright and lemony, yellow adapts easily to many color schemes. Combined with greens, it's summery. Use it with black, and it's sophisticated. Use it with red and orange, and it's hot and lively.

Yellow is the color we tend to notice before any others because it's highly reflective and gets our attention in the same way a bright light does. It's thought that it's the first color babies notice. It's also the reason why yellow is used for road signs to warn us to slow down or use caution.

In the home, yellow works well in any room where you want to feel uplifted and energized. Because of its reflective properties, yellow tends to appear brighter than white and is a good color for rooms that don't have enough light. And because it brings warmth to any room, it's a good choice in north-facing rooms to counteract the effect of cool northern light. While the light-infused versions of yellow are attention getters, the duller versions, including golds, tans, and some browns, are not as reflective. They are the more earthy versions of yellow that can often work as neutrals in a room, blending well with a variety of other colors.

◄ USING RED AS AN accent gives this kitchen and eating area a focal point and adds visual variety against the expanse of yellow. Because the yellow is so reflective, it would be glaring without the red accent on the wall.

▲ LOTS OF VIVID YELLOW gives this sunroom a jolt of sunshine from both inside and out. A space like this can easily take on other accent colors, which can change the mood of the room.

◄ THINK LEMONS AND LIMES in this family room. Because green and yellow are next to each other on the color wheel, they make a pleasing combination. Yellow is used again for the pillow on the sofa to link the space together.

Yellows

Yellow, the color that reminds us most of sunlight, can range from bright and glaring to soft and golden. Finding the right shade of yellow paint for your home can be challenging because the colors are often too bright and harsh, so instead think about using yellow in window treatments, upholstery, rugs, and accents.

► A PLEASANT COMBINATION of yellows, greens, and rosy hues gives this dining room a pretty look without overdoing the floral fabric. The soft green of the tablecloth is taken to a deeper hue on the windows for added emphasis.

◄ THIS YELLOW PANTRY area is set apart from the rest of the kitchen by color. In the kitchen beyond, the base cabinets are painted a lively lime green, while the upper cabinets are white. The green flooring connects the two areas with color.

Did You Know...

Legal pads are yellow for a reason. Behaviorally, yellow stimulates the mind and may help improve memory.

Sunny and Sophisticated

NOT TOO BRIGHT OR HARSH, these sunny yellows are pleasant and livable. Like the color of a ripe banana peel, many of these warm yellows could almost be considered neutrals. These timeless varieties go with nearly every color and combination of colors.

Creating a sophisticated room with yellow is an easy thing to do. If you want to use large amounts of the color, make sure you choose a soft version; otherwise the room will appear too bright. And as with any other color, view the shade on as large a sample board as possible, in good lighting and in the space. If you only want to add brighter yellow to a room in small amounts, combine it with white or off white for contrast, and bring in some darker elements such as darker wood furniture or metal finishes to help ground the space.

▼ THE WARMTH OF THE SUN is embraced in this light-filled sunroom. The analogous colors found in the rug were inspiration for the room and worked to tie in the terra-cotta tile flooring with the lighter palette of colors that includes yellow, greens, and white.

◄ YELLOW PAIRED WITH blue-gray makes for an inviting combination in this dining room. The yellow ceiling and draperies counteract any cooling effects the blue walls might impart. Both colors are brought together in the rug and the dining chair patterns.

▼ A SHEER YELLOW FABRIC softly filters the light entering this one-color breakfast room. Because the window fabric is the same color as the wall, it enhances the window. The white trim and white fabrics on the table and chairs provide subtle contrast.

Did You Know…

Many of the "standard" yellows that paint companies offer are often too harsh for large areas. Yellow that's similar to the color of butter works best in larger areas in most homes; brighter yellows work better as accents.

Earthy

THINK ABOUT THE COLOR of straw or sand and mix it with a little dirt, and you'll come up with earthy yellows. These muted golden and camel hues have brown undertones, so they work well in homes that contain dark or stained woodwork because all the elements feel natural. They also may contain small amounts of orange, giving them a slightly coppery or peachy quality. While these yellows are dulled-down they still add necessary light and a touch of brightness without being harsh.

▲ GOLDEN, FAUX FINISHED WALLS give this powder room character. The painted trim and black carpet add needed contrast and keep the room from looking bland.

◄ THE MONOCHROMATIC COLORS here range from a pale, creamy ivory to a mid-value gold, and contribute to a calm feeling room. The heavy texture of the stone provides visual interest.

◄ THIS YELLOW STAIRWAY seems to pull the sunshine right in. The black iron leaf and vine wall sconce work well with the birch railing, giving the whole stairway a nature-inspired look.

▼ GOLDEN WALLS SOFTEN the lines of the cherry woodwork and cabinetry in this Craftsman style kitchen. A variety of patterned pillows on the window seat provides additional color and texture and repeats the brown tones of the woodwork. If the walls had been painted white, the effect would be stark and not as inviting.

Classic and Traditional

CLASSIC, MID-TONE YELLOWS HAVE BEEN popular for many years. These are the pleasing and safe hues that never go out of style. Because they aren't trendy, these shades work well with traditional style furnishings. The light-reflective properties combine well with dark, 18th-century furnishings or rooms that have dark wood floors or trim. They also complement rooms with painted woodwork, giving those spaces a light, fresh quality. Often used with floral fabrics, these yellows work well with greens, reds, and blues for a timeless English look. When these yellows are used with oranges or purples, they tend to look more contemporary and lose their classic quality.

To add sophistication to a traditional style room, use one of these yellows with just one other color, like black or blue. This will increase the contrast and help the room make a dramatic statement.

▲ YELLOW AND WHITE plus black give this spectacular hallway an even more impressive look. If the walls had been left white, the results would not be as stunning. The black adds drama and contrast to the yellow without making the space seem dark. Because yellow reflects light, it's a good color for any room where you want to bring in light.

◀ BLACK, YELLOW, RED, AND WHITE are usually thought of as contemporary colors, but this room is very traditional thanks to the detailing and furniture style.

Did You Know...

Don't overlook your ceilings as a place to put color and show your creativity. Complementary colors often make for the most interesting look, while tonal combinations tend to be more soothing.

▼ YELLOW AND WHITE, this time with blue accents, makes for a time-tested color combination. The blue stone surrounding the fireplace was the obvious inspiration for the blue accent color. Without the yellow, the room would have been cold and uninviting.

▲ BECAUSE THEY WERE SET so high on the wall, these yellow wall tiles take on more impact in this bathroom. The retro feeling is enhanced by the black tile banding. The blue ceiling helps to cool down the large amount of warmth from the yellow tiles.

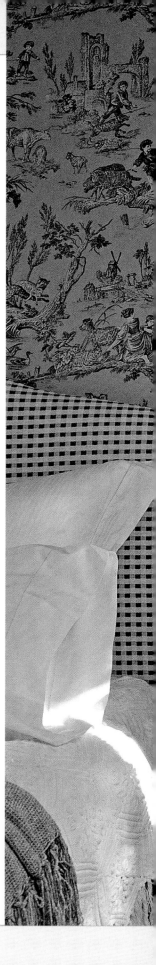

COLOR SCHEMES THAT WORK

Perfectly balanced in scale, three different patterns work here to make this room appealing and give it variety. The yellow-and-blue toile fabric that decorates the walls and windows is heavy, so the color scheme is balanced by the chair and headboard accents.

A HANDSOME plaid is introduced on the chair, repeating the exact blue and yellow colors as those found in the drapes. Because the scale of the plaid is large and the pattern is bold and geometric, it works well with the pattern on the walls and draperies.

A SMALLER SCALE check in the same blue color is used on the headboard, adding a third pattern.

A TRADITIONAL blue on yellow toile de Jouy pattern used for the draperies also covers the walls. Using a pattern like this, even on the ceiling, is a time-tested way of giving a room a consistent look.

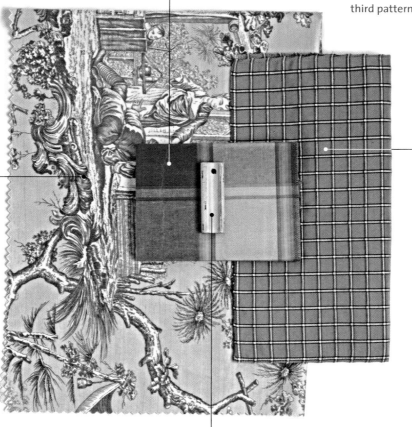

EVEN THE WARM yellow color of the chest has a relationship to the color scheme. Whether your wood furniture pieces are painted or stained, they have color. Because it has a similar tone to the background of the fabric and wallpaper, this chest blends and does not compete the way a white painted chest would have.

Strong and Bold

MUSTARD, SAFFRON, and other strong yellows work well with any style of home and furnishings, though they can be too harsh when used in large amounts unless the color is interrupted with another color or two. These yellows need to be tamed, so patterned fabrics that include a multitude of colors pair nicely with them. Equally important is the use of artwork, especially if the strong yellow color is on the walls. Large paintings or prints help the yellow to recede slightly because they draw the attention away from the wall color.

In a traditional setting, combine mustard yellow with deep blue. In a contemporary room, strong yellows pair well with pinks, purples, and reds, though they work best when used sparingly. Since these shades of yellow sometimes make skin tones a sickly greenish color, they shouldn't be used in bathrooms.

▲ BOLD PRIMARY COLORS comprise this whimsical room where yellow dominates. Because the colors are used with lots of white, they don't overpower the room; the soft neutral green accents give the eye a place to rest.

▶ STRONG YELLOW WALLS add a sunny, friendly look to this room. With this much yellow, the dark furniture is necessary for contrast and to add visual weight to the room.

THE BRIGHT YELLOW that covers two traditional French chairs contrasts vividly against black walls and dramatic contemporary artwork. This is a good example of one of Chevreul's Laws, that light colors appear more striking against black or dark colors.

Fresh

Fresh yellows are pure and clean because they don't contain any dull undertones. Whether lemony, pale, or nearly white, these yellows are full of light and remind us of summer and warmth.

If you want to create the illusion of more space, use lemon yellow on the walls to harness the color of the sun. This is a particularly effective color for rooms without windows or where you want the appearance of more light. If you're working with a room that has low ceilings, try yellow on the ceiling to open up the space. A very pale, almost white-yellow provides creaminess, and on wood trim adds subtle color that pure white can't provide. This creamy yellow also provides warmth when used on walls in a room with stained trim.

While fresh yellows work well with most other colors, they tend to fight with taupes and browns because of their contradicting qualities. Experiment with samples and swatches of different color combinations before committing to an entire color scheme.

▲ THIS LIVELY, CONTEMPORARY ROOM uses primary colors for impact. Yellow, red, and deep blue form the triadic scheme that has lots of energy and visual impact. The large painting on the wall, the red sofa, and patterned rug give the impression of creativity and fun.

Did You Know...

Reinforce a room's color scheme by using the same color as your wall color to line draperies or bedding. Just make sure the colors match.

▲ THOUGHT TO BE THE FIRST color that babies can see, yellow is gender-friendly and can be combined easily with other colors. The yellow ceiling keeps the warmth throughout this space.

◀ THE SYMMETRICAL arrangement of this room calls attention to the yellow cabinet in the center, balanced by the blue wood trim around the windows. This look is freshened by the contemporary window treatment that uses a good dose of white.

Neutrals

Decorating your home with lots of color means wearing your taste on your sleeve. That's why so many people choose neutrals instead. Using neutrals in your home isn't a bad thing; in fact, we actually need neutrals in our homes to make peace with all the other colors.

Although the word "neutral" implies lack of color, neutrals really are colors. The long held belief that neutrals are the easiest colors to work with is false. Any interior designer will tell you that neutrals are trickier to work with than other colors because neutrals are not really neutral! Just as with other colors, there are neutral color families and also neutral tones and tints within each color family. And sometimes the differences within the tones and tints are very subtle. For this reason it's hard to tell which neutrals are warm and which are cool until you compare them with other neutrals.

As with all colors, variations in neutrals can occur simply by changing textures. A heavily textured fabric will appear darker than the same color as a smooth fabric. That's because the light reflects off smooth surfaces, making them appear lighter. On a heavily textured surface, light is absorbed, making it appear darker than it really is. The differences in texture also work to make a neutral room more interesting. Combinations of textures that are smooth and shiny, matte and dull, and fine and heavy all contribute to a room's overall design quality and appeal.

ONE DARK BROWN WALL functions as an accent in this living room so as not to take away from the view out the window. If the window wall had been painted the same color, the room would have felt closed in. The white sofa provides contrast.

MOODMAKERS

Neutrals

Neutrals are colors, too. Neutrals can range from the thousands of whites to the deepest, darkest blacks, and everything in between. Beige, taupe, brown, and gray, and their thousands of variations are what we call neutrals. Dark neutrals add drama and contrast, while mid-tone and lighter neutrals are needed to separate colors and give our eyes a rest.

▲ FRESH AS THE OUTDOORS, this all-white bedroom is cool, thanks in part to the light blue ceiling and light-colored paint on the armoire. The metal bed frame helps to ground the room and keep it from feeling too cold.

▶ ASIDE FROM A SUBTLE pattern in the area rug, this neutral room gets its strength through contrast of light (the walls) and dark (the furnishings and shades).

KEEPING THE WALL and woodwork color similar to each other gives a room a subtle, understated look that calls attention to the other elements of the room, including the detailed fireplace mantel and wall art. Even the furnishings add subtle tone and texture.

IF BLACK WALLS seem too bold for you, try black accents for impact. Black would have been too heavy as the background color in this small powder room, but the accents add sophistication without being overpowering.

White

SINCE IT'S ALMOST ALWAYS associated with cleanliness, purity, and innocence, white is a good choice for kitchens, bathrooms, and bedrooms. Because white fabrics and carpets aren't always practical with kids and pets, you may want to use it for woodwork and accents, or areas where there's little chance of soiling. There is really no such thing as true white since true white is what appears whitest when compared to other whites. What this means in an all-white color scheme is that various tones of white can be introduced to help add variety and warmth, since an all-white room that uses bright whites looks sterile. White can take on tints of other colors that may look cool or warm, so for best results combine whites that have similar warmness or coolness. White needs some contrast and depth, which works best when scattered throughout a room to help relax the look.

▲ CREAMY YELLOW IS A GOOD CHOICE for a bathroom where there are no windows because it simulates sunlight. Combine yellow with white and any room will look bright and fresh.

◀ ACCENTS ARE IMPORTANT in an all-white room, and they're also easy to change with your mood. The bed is obviously the focal point, thanks in part to the dark frame, but the colored accents also pop against the white background.

Did You Know...

When decorating an all-white room, bring in warm wood tones to help keep the room from looking cold. This is easily accomplished with a wood floor, but also can be effective with furniture and accessories.

▲ THIS DINING ROOM contains so much dark woodwork that it almost demands white to keep it from becoming too heavy. The glass tabletop helps to reflect the white table base and chairs, and it reflects the white ceiling.

◄ THE RED, BLUE, AND GREEN painted furniture add color to this all-white room. Because there's no contrast between the white trim and the white walls, the eye doesn't stop but rather looks beyond the room's interior to the view outside.

Gray

WHEN USED SPARINGLY and in pale shades, gray can have a peaceful, calming effect on a room. But when silvery, smooth finishes are used, the room can take on a cool, clinical feel. Regardless of which shade of gray you choose, be wary of its negative effects—it's often linked to depression, especially the deeper, muddier tones.

On the positive side, colors that balance gray tend to be from the warm side of the color wheel. Orange, yellow, and red add liveliness and heat. If you live in a cool climate, even the warmer, lighter shades of gray look better when paired with warm colors to keep the color scheme from being too sterile.

As with beige, texture and contrast are important when creating a color scheme that revolves around gray. You may want to limit the use of gray by using it on small furniture items, not walls. It's also important to make sure a room that features a good dose of gray has plenty of natural or artificial light to help warm it up.

▲ A LARGE AMOUNT of blue-gray slate provides a contemporary, cool feeling in this bathroom. The wood tones of the cabinet drawers add a touch of warmth.

▲ GRAY WALLS and dining chairs make this simple, one-color scheme look sophisticated and subdued. The dramatic artwork is emphasized thanks to the neutral walls. The light wood tones of the furniture add warmth that counteracts any coolness of the gray.

◄ IN THIS DINING ROOM, the white trim pops out against the soft gray walls. If the walls and trim were the same color, much of the room's character would be lost.

▲ A COOL, MID-VALUE GRAY and warm neutrals combine in this bedroom for a monotone scheme that is freshened by the white woodwork and white background of the bedding. The large amount of white keeps the room from feeling too gloomy, which can happen when a healthy dose of gray is used.

COLOR SCHEMES THAT WORK

The interior design of open spaces like this can be approached from two different perspectives: Use color to highlight furnishings, or keep things neutral inside to focus on a view outside. In this room, both are accomplished because the color scheme isn't too strong.

THE WALL COLOR, because it's painted in a similar tone to the floor, expands the space and brings continuity from the walls and ceiling to the floor.

A GRAY, mid-value textured fabric is a good choice on such a large piece of furniture because it blends rather than stands out in the room and allows the architecture of the room to be more prominent.

TWO LEATHER chairs, covered in a reddish-brown color, add contrast as well as color to the room.

A THROW in the same reddish color as the chairs distributes that bold color throughout the room.

THE BLEACHED wood floor that runs throughout the space gives this house a light quality.

IN A ROOM with a view like this, using busy patterns would be a mistake because they would detract from the view. The rug functions to connect the colors of the room together because it features the gray and red, colors that are used on the furniture. In addition, the area rug is space-defining, setting the boundaries of the conversation area and holding the furniture arrangement together.

Beige

IF YOU LOVE THE LOOK OF CLEAN, understated design, a restricted color palette could be the look you're after. Beige, basically a variation of white, gives a room a light, simple look that sits in the background and lets everything else in the room command attention. The lines of the furnishings become emphasized in a beige room, so it's better to use bold shapes rather than frilly details when using a lot of beige in your color scheme. Beige also provides an excellent background for art, sculpture, or antiques and unique furniture.

Most colors goes well with beige, so think about what you want your color scheme to accomplish. Black accents add dramatic appeal, while bold, bright colors introduce vitality. If you want to use other pale colors, be sure to introduce contrast in the way of texture and value changes so that the room isn't boring. Texture can come from fabrics on furniture, window treatments, and accessories or through the use of accent pieces, lamps, and plants.

▲ MANY ROOMS WITH A beige background require some element to take center stage in order to keep the room from being dull. Here, the art plays that role, as do the small windows peppering the wall.

◄ THE BEDROOM IS A GOOD PLACE for a quiet, restful color scheme like this one. The layered neutrals don't demand much visual attention. The soft, blush-colored throw makes a nice addition that keeps the scheme calm and flatters skin tones.

TAUPE, A NEUTRAL, is not actually one specific color, but a generic term used to define any of thousands of neutrals that are not really beige, brown, or gray, but any mixture of those colors.

THE COLORS OF THE WOOD trim, mantel, and beams have similar tones to those in the stone. Because these colors do not contrast each other, the room has a quiet, relaxing look.

COLOR SCHEMES THAT WORK

All-neutral rooms demand the use of texture and contrast to keep them from looking boring. Here, a combination of all-neutral fabrics are made interesting by wood and bamboo finishes.

OTHER FABRICS, like this smaller scale check, can be added, providing yet more diversity in the pattern while keeping the color scheme the same.

DECORATIVE TRIM adds texture and movement on any pillow or window treatment, but are especially effective in one-color scheme.

BAMBOO is a textural material, so while the color is within the beige family, the material itself brings in a touch of nature.

THE PLAID window treatment fabric combines the same shades of neutrals used in the pillow fabrics in a geometric pattern. The plaid makes the brown more dominant on the windows, adding visual weight to that part of the room.

A TONAL, floral fabric containing several shades of neutrals was used for the pillows.

THE HEADBOARD and wall sconces, finished in the same worn driftwood tone, keep some consistency among the hard elements of the room and help the space to stay cohesive. If these pieces were of two different materials or finishes, the look would have been more disparate.

Did You Know...

Contrast commands attention, so if that's not what you want, use similar colors in a decorating scheme to de-emphasize the contrast.

▼ THE TRADITIONAL DEEP BEIGE color on the cabinetry and woodwork blends well with the terra-cotta tile floor, and gives the cabinets more of an architectural presence in the room. The color allows for almost unlimited possibilities for accent colors.

◄ DRAMA CAN BE FOUND in even a neutral color scheme, as evidenced by this sophisticated living room. The architectural features contribute to the feeling but they are enhanced by the warm background color and accents of red, black, and golden yellow.

▲ IF YOU THINK BEIGE is boring, look again. The black screen behind the sofa adds drama. Any other strong color, such as dark brown, deep purple, or dark red would have provided similar results.

◄ THIS MONOTONE COLOR scheme incorporates only one color family and creates a tranquil atmosphere. A blended palette of warm beige tones and minimal pattern works well with the painted woodwork. A slightly deeper tone of the same color is used for the carpeting.

Brown

MOST OF US ALREADY HAVE brown in our home because it's usually the color of wood. Look at your furniture and you'll probably see many shades of brown, ranging from rich walnut to reddish brown cherry tones, or golden-brown hues. The brown tones in your furniture can be enhanced by forming a color scheme around them, or left to stand on their own.

Brown gives the feeling of permanence, so it provides stability and security. It's considered a neutral color because it contrasts with most other colors. Dark, rich brown, which provides an effect similar to black but isn't as harsh, adds drama to a room. Midtone, chocolate browns add warmth and depth and work well with red, gold, and green. In lighter values, brown moves toward taupe and gold colors, and requires stronger colors to keep a room from feeling too boring.

▲ THIS CHAIR WAS BOUGHT before the walls were painted. The wall color was chosen to match the chair upholstery to take the focus off the furniture and make the architectural elements of the room the primary focus.

◀ RED AND BROWN COMBINE to create a warm, rich look. The dark walls emphasize the wall art, the color of which is repeated in the floral print chair and ottoman. The pattern and golden color prevent the room from having too much contrast.

◄ ONE DARK BROWN WALL provides a sense of richness to this bathroom. Because the other walls use the dark brown on the bottom half only and a lighter neutral on the top half, the room feels cohesive.

▼ MID-VALUE CHOCOLATE BROWN walls and a darker brown sofa and chair make this monochromatic room a space where the colors are blended, not contrasted. Light wood trim and carpeting keep the room from looking dark.

◀ THE NATURAL MAPLE CABINETS take up so much wall space that almost any dark color would enhance the feel of the room. As a good rule, repeat the wall color in some of the furnishings, as was done here.

▼ SURROUNDED BY LIGHT, this kitchen banquette easily handles the warm brown, which helps to define the seating area. Lots of white trim keeps the space fresh and adds contrast.

▲ DON'T BE AFRAID TO try deep colors in small spaces. These deep butterscotch-colored walls add richness that provides a good backdrop for traditional art. The chrome fixtures add light and sparkle.

Did You Know...

Flat paint absorbs light while glossy paint reflects it. Experiment with sheen levels to get the effect you're after.

▲ BECAUSE ALL THE FURNITURE and woodwork have brown wood tones, sage green was used on the walls to add just enough interest. The reddish brown tones in the wood are enhanced by the green, which is the opposite color family.

▶ BECAUSE OF THE DARK COLORS of the wall and sofa and light colors in the artwork, you notice the art before you notice the furniture. Additionally, the vaulted ceiling stands out thanks to its light color.

COLOR SCHEMES THAT WORK

A combination of brown, blue, and neutrals uses color in a modern way. The light and dark, plus one strong accent color, makes for an easy to create color scheme that guarantees success.

THE PLAIN sofa fabric has no pattern but it does have a lot of texture. The shade of white was chosen to match the white in the brown print. If the two fabrics weren't coordinated, the white might have looked yellow, gray, or green with the other colors in the room.

A CHOCOLATE brown print, used just on one chair, establishes the contrast to the neutrals.

A FUZZY, BLUE chenille throw contributes the blue accent color.

THE BARREL chair covered in a tweedy fabric adds a bit more brown to the scheme, but its primary responsibility is to add texture to the room.

BLUE PILLOWS in the same color as the throw also provide accent. Because they are placed opposite the throw, the color is balanced on both ends of the sofa.

ACCESSORIES ON the bookcase repeat the accent color. This repetition of color is an effective way to build a successful color scheme.

Black

BLACK ADDS INSTANT PRESENCE to any room and completely changes the feeling of a space based on the amount used. When combined with other colors, black is powerful. Alone, it's unapproachable and intimidating. Although black is traditionally associated with death, it is also an elegant color that suggests worldliness, dignity, and mystery.

Because black *seems* to lack any color, it goes with everything. Small touches of black can easily be brought in to most rooms and can work to connect adjacent rooms. A black iron base on a table, a black lamp shade, a black marble top on a chest, or a black pillow are suggestions for using black in small ways. On a larger scale, a black leather chair or sofa, an area rug that contains large amounts of black, or even black walls can give a room a strong and dramatic look.

▲ DEEP, DARK CABINETS contrast against the lighter wood floor. The cool, pale, blue-green color chosen for the wall color emphasizes the cabinetry and reinforces the contemporary look.

◄ THIS BLACK LEATHER SOFA is softened by the patterned fabric on the seat cushions, providing texture and color. The fabrics and the rug both contain small amounts of the golden-orange color that inspired the wall color.

▲ IN THIS CONTEMPORARY dining room, black and cream comprise this simple, yet dramatic scheme. Even the cornice across the top of the window, as well as the cove molding along the ceiling are black. The texture of the floor covering is essential because of all the smooth surfaces in the room.

◄ BLACK WALLS MIGHT BE out of the question in some rooms, but not here. Since this room has so much light and wide woodwork, the black wall is stunning. And since black also appears in the rug, uphol- stery, and fireplace, the room is cohesive.

COLOR SCHEMES THAT WORK

Black and white is such a classic combination that any other color can be used as the accent. Here, the multiple patterns add an air of whimsy and energy and together create a room with personality. Combined with the yellow accent, the scheme is warm and inviting.

A BOLD CHECK fabric on the headboard, coverlet, and bed skirt takes the primary attention in this bedroom. The shape of the headboard helps to soften the straight lines on the fabric.

THE CHAIR is covered in a yellow textured fabric, establishing the accent color on the second largest piece of furniture in the room. The coverlet on the bed is lined with yellow, bringing the accent to the largest area of black in the room.

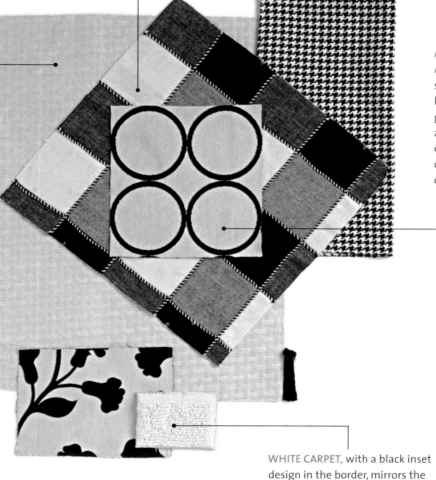

ASSORTED BLACK-AND-WHITE patterns, some with curved lines and some with geometric shapes, add contrast to the check fabric while continuing the color scheme.

WHITE CARPET, with a black inset design in the border, mirrors the shapes in the pillows.

Credits

CHAPTER 1

p. 4: (left) Photo © Eric Roth, courtesy *Inspired House,* © The Taunton Press, Inc.

p. 6: Photo © B rian Vanden Brink

p. 7: (top) Photo © Mark Lohman; (bottom) Photo © Steve Vierra

p.8: Photo © Sloan Howard

p.9: Photo © Karen Melvin; designer: Gigi Olive, Gigi Olive Interior Designs, Minneapolis

p. 10: Photo © davidduncanlivingston.com

p. 11: (top) Photo © Mark Lohman; (bottom) Photo Karen Tanaka, courtesy *Inspired House,* © The Taunton Press, Inc.

p. 12: (top) Photo © Eric Roth; design: Susan Sargent

p. 13: (top) Photo © Mark Samu; (bottom) Photo Mike Jensen, courtesy *Inspired House* © The Taunton Press, Inc.

p. 14: (top) Photo © Tim Street-Porter; (bottom) Photo © Jessie Walker

p. 15: Photo © Mark Lohman

p. 16: (top) Photo © Mark Lohman; (bottom) Photo © Steve Vierra

p. 17: Photo © Brian Vanden Brink

p. 18: Photo © Sloan Howard

p. 19: Photo © Eric Roth

CHAPTER 2

p. 20: Photo © Tim Street-Porter

p. 22: (top) Photo © Tim Street Porter; (bottom) Photo © Karen Melvin; design: Robin Strangis, ASID, Loring Interiors, Minneapolis, and Kim Spillum, Allied member ASID, Kim Spillum Interior Designs, Minneapolis

p. 23: (top) Photo © James Ray Spahn; (bottom) Photo © Mark Lohman

p. 24: Photo © Sloan Howard

p. 25: Photo © Eric Roth

p. 26: (top) Photo © Steve Vierra; design: Freya Senabian; (bottom) Photo courtesy Joel Koyama; design: Leslie Meyers, Partners 4, and Robin Strangis, ASID, Loring Interiors, Minneapolis

p. 28: (top) Photo © Jesse Walker

p. 29: (top) Photo © Steve Vierra; (bottom) Photo © Jesse Walker, Architect: Thomas L. Bosworth

p. 30: Photo © Sloan Howard

p. 31: Photo © Erik Roth

p. 32: (top) Photo © carolynbates.com; (bottom) Photo © Mark Samu

p. 33: Photo ©Brian Vanden Brink

p. 34: Photo © Sloan Howard

p. 35: Photo © Steve Vierra

CHAPTER 3

p. 36: Photo © Erik Roth

p. 38: (top) Photo © Tim Street-Porter; design Barbara Berry; (bottom) Photo © Erik Roth

p. 39: (top) Photo © Mark Lohman; (bottom) Photo © Tim Street-Porter

p. 40: (top) Photo © Mark Lohman; (bottom) Photo © davidduncanlivingston.com

p. 41: Photo © Steve Vierra

p. 42: Photo © Mark Lohman

p. 43: Photo © Randy O'Rourke

p. 44: Photo © Sloan Howard

p. 45: Photo © Karen Melvin; design: Gigi Olive, Gigi Olive Interiors LLC, Minneapolis

p. 46: (top) Photo © Eric Roth; design: Susan Sargeant; (bottom) Photo © Steve Vierra

p. 47: (top) Photo © Eric Roth; (bottom) Photo © Eric Roth; design: Susan Sargeant

p. 48: Photo © Sloan Howard

p. 49: Photo © Evan Sklar

p. 50: (top) Photo © Eric Roth; (bottom) Photo © Mark Lohman

p. 51: Photo © Tim Street-Porter

p. 52: (top) Photo © Eric Roth; (bottom) Photo courtesy The Sherwin Williams Company

p. 53: Photo © Mark Lohman

CHAPTER 4

p. 54: Photo © davidduncanlivingston.com

p. 56: (top) Photo © Jessie Walker; (bottom) Need photographer; design: Katie Sidenberg, Minneapolis

p. 57: (left) Photo © Tim Street-Porter; (right) Photo © davidduncanlivingston.com, James W. Givens Designs

p. 58: Photo © Eric Roth; Design: Susan Sargent

p. 59: (right & left) Photos © Jessie Walker

p. 60: Photo © Steve Vierra

p. 61: (top) Photo © Dana Wheelock, Wheelock Photography; design: Katie Sidenberg, Robert Sidenberg, Inc., Minneapolis; (bottom) Photo © Roger Turk/ Northlight Photography, Design: Carleen Cafferty Interiors

p. 62: Photo © Sloan Howard

p. 63: Photo © Mark Lohman

p. 64: (top) Photo © davidduncanlivingston.com; (bottom) Photo courtesy The Sherwin Williams Company

p. 65: (left) Photo © Mark Lohman; (right) Photo © Mark Samu

p. 66: Photo © davidduncanlivingston.com

p. 67: (right) Photo © Eric Roth; left: Photo © carolynbates.com; design: The Cushman Design Group; General Contractor: Patterson & Smith Construction

p. 68: (right) Photo © Mark Lohman; (left) Photo © davidduncanlivingston.com

p. 69: (top) Photo © Eric Roth; (bottom) Photo © Jessie Walker

p. 70: Photo © Mark Samu

p. 71: (left) Photo courtesy The Sherwin Williams Company; (right) Photo © davidduncanlivingston.com

p. 72: (top & bottom) Photos © Steve Vierra

p. 73: (top) Photo © Jessie Walker; (bottom) Photo © Karen Melvin, Interior designers: Robin Strangis, ASID, Loring Interiors, Minneapolis, and Kim Spillum, Allied Member, ASID, Kim Spillum Interior Designs, Minneapolis

p. 74: Photo © Sloan Howard

p. 75: Photo © Steve Vierra; design: Decorative Interiors

CHAPTER 5

p. 76: Photo © Tim Street-Porter

p. 78: (top) Photo © Bruce Buck; (bottom) Photo © davidduncanlivingston.com

p. 79: Photo © Eric Roth

p. 80: (top) Photo courtesy The Sherwin Williams Company; (bottom) Photo © Eric Roth

p. 81: (top) Photo © Lee Anne White; design: Robin Cowley, Color Consultant; (middle) Photo © Steve Vierra; (bottom) Photo © Eric Roth

p. 82: Photo © davidduncanlivingston.com

p. 83: (top) Photo © Brian Vanden Brink; (middle) Photo © Eric Roth; design: Susan Sargent; (bottom) Photo © Eric Roth

p. 84: Photo © Sloan Howard

p. 85: Photo © Eric Roth

p. 86: Photo © Steve Vierra

p. 87: (top & bottom) Photos © davidduncanlivingston.com

p. 88: (top) Photo © Eric Roth; (bottom) Photo © Brian Vanden Brink

p. 89: Photo © davidduncanlivingston.com

CHAPTER 6

p. 90: Photo © Tim Street-Porter

p. 92: (top) Photo © Steve Vierra; (bottom) Photo © Jessie Walker

p. 93: Photo © davidduncanlivingston.com

p. 94: Photo © Mark Lohman

p. 95: (left) Photo © davidduncanlivingston.com; (right) Photo © Jessie Walker

p. 96: Photo © davidduncanlivingston.com

p. 97: (top & bottom left) Photos © Eric Roth; (bottom right) Photo © Steve Vierra

p. 98 (top) Photo © Steve Vierra; (bottom) Photo © Brian Vanden Brink

p. 99: Photo © Jessie Walker

p. 100: (top) Photo © Steve Vierra; (bottom) Photo © Mark Samu

p. 101: Photo © Mark Lohman

p. 102: Photo © Sloan Howard

p. 103: Photo © Steve Vierra

p. 104: (top) Photo © Mark Lohman; (bottom) Photo © davidduncanlivingston.com

p. 105: Photo © Philip Jensen-Carter; design: Carol J. W. Kurth, AIA, PC, www.carolkurtharchitects.com

p. 106 (top) Photo © James Ray Spahn; (bottom) Photo © Tim Street-Porter

p. 107: (top) Photo © Alise O'Brien; design: Directions in Design; (bottom) Photo © Jessie Walker

p. 108: Photo © Sloan Howard

p. 109: Photo © Eric Roth

CHAPTER 7

p. 110: Photo © Mark Lohman

p. 112: (top & bottom) Photo © Mark Lohman

p. 113: (left) Photo © Mark Lohman; (right) Photo © Steve Vierra

p. 114: Photo © Sloan Howard

p. 115: © Winfried Heinze, courtesy Inspired House

p. 116: (top) Photo © James Ray Spahn; (bottom) Photo © Jessie Walker

p. 117: (top) Photo © Eric Roth; Designer: Susan Sargent; (middle & bottom) Photos © Jessie Walker

p. 118: Photo © Sloan Howard

p. 119: Photo © Mark Samu

p. 120: (top) Photo © Mark Lohman; (bottom) Photo © davidduncanlivingston.com

p. 121: Photo © Tim Street-Porter

p. 122: Photo © Eric Roth

p. 123: (top right) Photo courtesy The Sherwin Williams Company; (top left & bottom right) Photos © davidduncanlivingston.com

p. 124: Photo © Mark Lohman

p. 125: (top) Photo © James Ray Spahn; (middle) Photo © Randy O'Rourke; (bottom) Photo © Eric Roth; designer: Susan Sargent

p. 126: Photo © Sloan Howard

p. 127: Photo courtesy The Sherwin Williams Company

CHAPTER 8

p. 128: Photo © Mark Lohman

p. 130: (left) Photo © Tim Street-Porter; (right) Photo © Jessie Walker

p. 131: Photo © Evan Sklar

p. 132: (top) Photo © davidduncanlivingston.com; bottom: Photo © Eric Roth Designer; Design: Susan Sargent

p. 133: Photo © Mark Lohman

p. 134: (left) Photo © Brian Vanden Brink; (right) Photo courtesy The Sherwin Williams Company

p. 135: (top) Photo © Eric Roth; (bottom) Photo © Mark Lohman

p. 136: Photo © Sloan Howard

p. 137: Photo © Eric Roth

p. 138: (top & bottom) Photos © Brian Vanden Brink

p. 139: Photo © Eric Roth

p. 140: (top) Photo © Karen Tanaka; (bottom) Photo © Eric Roth

p. 141: Photo courtesy Stickley

Fine Furniture

CHAPTER 9

p. 142: Photo © Eric Roth

p. 144: (left) Photo © Mark Lohman; (right) Photo © Jessie Walker

p. 145: (top) Photo © Steve Vierra; (bottom) Photo © Mark Lohman

p. 146: Photo © Karen Melvin, Interior designers; Robin Strangis, Loring Interiors, and Kim Spillum, Kim Spillum Interior Designs, Minneapolis

p. 147: (top) Photo © Mark Lohman; (bottom) Photo © Mark Samu

p. 148: (right) Photo © davidduncanlivingston.com; (left) Photo courtesy Stickley Fine Upholstery

p. 149: (top) Photo © Brian Vanden Brink; (bottom) Photo Karen Tanaka, courtesy *Inspired House*, © The Taunton Press, Inc.

p. 150: (top & bottom) Photos © Jessie Walker

p. 151: (top) Photo © Mark Samu; (bottom) Photo © Jessie Walker

p. 152: Photo © Sloan Howard

p. 153: Photo © Steve Vierra

p. 154: (top & bottom) Photos © davidduncanlivingston.com

p. 155: Photo © Jessie Walker

p. 156: Photo © Eric Roth

p. 157: (left) Photo © Mark Samu; (right) Photo © Jessie Walker

CHAPTER 10

p. 158: Photo © davidduncanlivingston.com

p. 160: (top) Photo © davidduncanlivingston.com; (bottom) Photo © Steve Vierra

p. 161: (top) Photo © Steve Vierra; (bottom) Photo © Jessie Walker

p. 162: (top) Photo © Jessie Walker; (bottom) Photo © davidduncanlivingston.com

p. 163: (top) Photo © Steve Vierra; (bottom) Photo © Jessie

Walker

p. 164: (top) Photo © carolynbates.com, Design Geoffrey Wolcott, GKW Working Designs; (middle) Photo © Steve Vierra; (bottom) Photo © Grey Crawford

p. 165: Photo © Greg Browning, EyeCandi

p. 166: Photo © Sloan Howard

p. 167: Photo © davidduncanlivingston.com

p. 168: (right) Photo © Brian Vanden Brink; (left) Photo © Steve Vierra

p. 169: (top) Photo © Mark Lohman; (bottom) Photo © Steve Vierra

p. 170: Photo © Sloan Howard

p. 171: Photo © Brian Vanden Brink

p. 172 (top) Photo © Jessie Walker; (bottom) Photo © Steve Vierra

p. 173: (top) Photo © Jessie Walker; (middle) Photo © Mark Lohman; (bottom) Photo © Steve Vierra

p. 174: (top) Photo courtesy The Sherwin Williams Company; (bottom) Photo © Jessie Walker

p. 175: (top & bottom) Photos © Steve Vierra

p. 176: (top right) Photo © Steve Vierra; (top left) Photo © Eric Roth; (bottom) Photo © Jessie Walker

p. 177: (top) Photo © Jessie Walker; (bottom) Photo © davidduncanlivingston.com

p. 178: Photo © Sloan Howard

p. 179: Photo © Greg Browning, EyeCandi

p. 180: (top) Photo © davidduncanlivingston.com; (bottom) Photo courtesy Stickley Fine Upholstery

p. 181: (top & bottom) Photos © Jessie Walker

p. 182: Photo © Sloan Howard

p. 183: Photo © Brian Vanden Brink

For More Great Design Ideas, Look for These and Other Taunton Press Books Wherever Books are Sold.

NEW KITCHEN IDEA BOOK
1-56158-693-5
Product #070773
$19.95 U.S./$27.95 Canada

NEW BATHROOM IDEA BOOK
1-56158-692-7
Product #070774
$19.95 U.S./$27.95 Canada

NEW KIDSPACE IDEA BOOK
1-56158-694-3
Product #070776
$19.95 U.S./$27.95 Canada

NEW BUILT-INS IDEA BOOK
1-56158-673-0
Product #070755
$19.95 U.S./$27.95 Canada

TRIM IDEA BOOK
1-56158-710-9
Product #070786
$19.95 U.S./$27.95 Canada

TILE IDEA BOOK
1-56158-709-5
Product #070785
$19.95 U.S./$27.95 Canada

STONESCAPING IDEA BOOK
1-56158-763-X
Product #070824
$14.95 U.S./$21.00 Canada

OUTDOOR LIVING IDEA BOOK
1-56158-757-5
Product #070820
$19.95 U.S./$27.95 Canada

ORGANIZING IDEA BOOK
1-56158-780-X
Product #070835
$14.95 U.S./$21.00 Canada

CURB APPEAL IDEA BOOK
1-56158-803-2
Product #070853
$19.95 U.S./$27.95 Canada

TAUNTON'S HOME STORAGE IDEA BOOK
1-56158-676-5
Product #070758
$19.95 U.S./$27.95 Canada

TAUNTON'S FAMILY HOME IDEA BOOK
1-56158-729-X
Product #070789
$19.95 U.S./$27.95 Canada

TAUNTON'S HOME WORKSPACE IDEA BOOK
ISBN 1-56158-701-X
Product #070783
$19.95 U.S./$27.95 Canada

BACKYARD IDEA BOOK
1-56158-667-6
Product #070749
$19.95 U.S./$27.95 Canada

POOL IDEA BOOK
1-56158-764-8
Product #070825
$19.95 U.S./$27.95 Canada

BABYSPACE IDEA BOOK
1-56158-799-0
Product #070857
$14.95 U.S./$21.00 Canada

DECORATING IDEA BOOK
1-56158-762-1
Product #070829
$24.95 U.S./$34.95 Canada

WINDOW TREATMENT IDEA BOOK
1-56158-819-9
Product #070869
$19.95 U.S./$26.95 Canada